PIL...

(TAGALOG)
PHRASEBOOK

Violetta Lorenzana

Pilipino (Tagalog) phrasebook
  2nd edition

Published by
  Lonely Planet Publications
  Head Office: PO Box 617, Hawthorn, Vic 3122, Australia
  Branches: 155 Filbert Street, Suite 251, Oakland CA 94607, USA
                    10a Spring Place, London NW5 3BH, UK
                    71 bis rue de Cardinal Lemoine, 75005 Paris, France

Printed by
Colorcraft Ltd, Hong Kong

Cover Illustration
Jeepney Up Scotty by Han Than Tun

Published
  April 1998

National Library of Australia Cataloguing in Publication Data

Lorenzana, Violetta, 1944-
  Pilipino (Tagalog) phrasebook
  2nd ed.
  Includes index.
  ISBN 0 86442 432 9.

  1. Tagalog language -- Conversation and phrase books – English. I.
  Title. (Series : Lonely Planet language survival kit).

  499.21183421

© Lonely Planet Publications Pty Ltd, 1998
Cover Illustration © Lonely Planet

About the Author

Violetta Lorenzana has a Bachelor of Science degree in Foreign Service from the University of the Philippines in Quezon City.

She lived in Germany for two years while her mother was a Minister Counsellor in the Philippine Embassy in Bonn.

She finished the Studrenkolleg in order to study at Bonn University where she took Spanish, Italian, French and Russian.

She taught German at Philippine Science High School, Manila Science High School and the Goethe Institute in Manila for 15 years. Violetta also worked as a translator from German to English and vice-versa in the Philippines.

She taught Pilipino at the Council for Adult Education in Melbourne and is currently working as a contract interpreter and translator. Violetta is married and has five children.

From the Author

The author wishes to thank her mother, Inay, for helping with the grammar section, her daughter, Arabella, her sisters, Bong and Lina, her niece, Prissy Ann, her sister-in-law, Gina, a friend, Renee, all of whom helped in the preparation of this phrasebook. Special thanks to her husband, Chito, for helpful discussions about phrases and words.

From the Publisher

This book was put together by a number of fine and noble people. Peter D'Onghia edited it while discovering the finer points of juniper berries. Sally Steward oversaw the production of it but was disappointed to find that drinking San Miguel beer doesn't get you closer to heaven. Fabrice Rocher managed to juggle catching frogs with laying out the book. Penelope Richardson, whose dreams of driving a canary yellow jeepney ended in tears and an empty bottle, designed the book. Diana Saad proofread. Richard Plunkett supplied the confounding crossword clues and a touch of class. Han Than Tun drew the wonderful illustrations and cover and Adam McCrow put the cover together and proved that blondes have more fun.

The publisher wishes to thank Jens Peters who kindly gave us permission to use small pieces from his Lonely Planet guidebook to the Philippines.

Thanks to Dr. John U. Wolff, Professor of Linguistics and Asian Studies at Cornell University, New York, who wrote the first edition of the Lonely Planet Pilipino phrasebook, from which this edition developed.

CONTENTS

INTRODUCTION

Pilipino, or as it is more commonly known, Tagalog, is one of two official languages of the Philippines. English, the other official language, is used, along with Pilipino, for most business, governmental and legal transactions.

In the Philippines, there are approximately 100 regional languages or dialects spoken and Tagalog ranks as the principal regional language. Tagalog's grammar is not always interpretable in terms of Latin-based grammars. It is, however, easily understandable, particularly to people who are familiar with Malayo-Polynesian languages. It's a member of the Malayo-Polynesian language family whose members are spread from Madagascar to Tonga. It has words from the other Philippine dialects, as well as words which show Sanskrit and Arabic influences. Identifiable also, are Chinese and Spanish words. This is not surprising because trade relations with the Chinese, the Arabs and other Islamic seafaring merchants were conducted well before the time of the second wave of Spanish colonisers. The Spanish colonisers stayed for over three centuries and gave the Filipinos the Catholic religion and many Spanish words, found not only in Tagalog but also in the other dialects. Pilipino, in its present form, also contains many Spanish and English words spelled the Pilipino way.

Originally, Tagalog was spoken only in Manila and the nearby areas of what are now the provinces of Rizal, Bulacan, Cavite, Nueva Ecija, Quezon, Batangas, Mindoro and Laguna. The learning of Tagalog as a compulsory subject in the primary and the secondary schools has contributed to its expansive use all over the country with almost every Filipino, speaking and understanding it, to some extent. At present, lectures in the universities can be given in English, Pilipino or a mixture of both languages, depending upon the lecturer, the students and the subject being studied. Students may recite in either language as they choose. People from other language regions gravitate towards Manila, not only because of its social significance, but also because of better employment opportunities. The contribution of mass media – radio, television, films, newspapers and magazines – to the spread of Tagalog cannot be overlooked.

In 1937, Tagalog was declared the official national language of the Philippines because it was the dialect spoken in the capital city, Manila, and was already generally understood and spoken by most Filipinos. Historically, it was also the language used by the leaders of the Philippine revolution against Spanish rule, since most of them were from Tagalog-speaking regions. The most notable among them is Jose Rizal, the national hero, who was from Laguna. Much later, in view of expressed protest by other language regions, the National Language Institute declared that Tagalog was merely to be the basis of the national language while it borrowed words from the other regional languages. People speaking these other regional languages, however, claimed that the language was simply Tagalog with a sprinkling of the other dialects. To appease such complaints, the official national language was renamed Pilipino, a more encompassing term. The objective was to make the new name more acceptable to Filipinos of non-Tagalog regions.

Most Filipinos can speak and understand both Pilipino and English and are generally friendly and hospitable. Travellers will find that getting around, even outside of the cities, will not be difficult.

GETTING STARTED

Pilipino and English are widely spoken in the Philippines. As you go through the phrasebook you will see the influence of English and Spanish in the words commonly used in everyday language. Most of them have Pilipino counterparts, of course, but using them in conversation could sound stilted or artificial. Synonyms of the words have been given. For conversation purposes, it is best to use the words derived from Spanish or English, particularly if you are speaking to a young person or someone from the Manila area. You'll find English words within some phrases. These are words with which an average Filipino is likely to be familiar. They may also be new words specially used for certain fields, such as photography and computer terms which as yet have no Pilipino counterparts.

In Pilipino, you can speak in the polite or informal form. It is explained in the phrasebook when to use one or the other. It is also indicated in the phrasebook which form has been used in the list of phrases under the headings. However, where there is no indication, the phrases are given in the polite form only.

Abbreviations Used in This Book

art	article	m	masculine
col	colloquial	n	noun
f	feminine	pl	plural
fam	familiar	pol	polite
lit	literally	sg	singular

HOW TO USE THIS PHRASEBOOK
You *Can* Speak Another Language

It's true – anyone can speak another language. Don't worry if you haven't studied languages before, or that you studied a language at school for years and can't remember any of it. It doesn't even matter if you failed English grammar. After all, that's never affected your ability to speak English! And this is the key to picking

INTRODUCTION

up a language in another country. You don't need to sit down and memorise endless grammatical details and you don't need to memorise long lists of vocabulary. You just need to start speaking. Once you start, you'll be amazed how many prompts you'll get to help you build on those first words. You'll hear people speaking, pick up sounds from TV, catch a word or two that you think you know from the local radio, see something on a billboard – all these things help to build your understanding.

Plunge In

There's just one thing you need to start speaking another language – courage. Your biggest hurdle is overcoming the fear of saying aloud what may seem to you to be just a bunch of sounds.

The best way to start overcoming your fear is to memorise a few key words. These are the words you know you'll be saying again and again, like 'hello', 'thank you' and 'how much?'. Here's an important hint though: right from the beginning, learn at least one phrase that will be useful but not essential. Such as 'good morning' or 'good afternoon', 'see you later' or even a conversational piece like 'lovely day, isn't it?' or 'it's cold today' (people everywhere love to talk about the weather). Having this extra phrase (just start with one, if you like, and learn to say it really well) will enable you to move away from the basics, and when you get a reply and a smile, it'll also boost your confidence. You'll find that people you speak to will like it too, as they'll understand that at least you've tried to learn more of the language than just the usual essential words.

Ways to Remember

There are several ways to learn a language. Most people find they learn from a variety of these, although people usually have a preferred way to remember. Some like to see the written word and remember the sound from what they see. Some like to just hear it spoken in context (if this is you, try talking to yourself in Pilipino, but do it in the car or somewhere private, to give yourself confidence, and so others don't wonder about your sanity!).

Others, especially the more mathematically inclined, like to analyse the grammar of a language, and piece together words according to the rules of grammar. The very visually inclined like to associate the written word and even sounds with some visual stimulus, such as from illustrations, TV and general things they see in the street. As you learn, you'll discover what works best for you – be aware of what made you really remember a particular word, and if it sticks in your mind, keep using that method.

Kicking Off

Chances are you'll want to learn some of the language before you go. The first thing to do is to memorise those essential phrases and words. Check out the basics (page 47) ... and don't forget that extra phrase (see Plunge In!). Try the sections on making conversation or greeting people for a phrase you'd like to use. Write some of these words down on a separate piece of paper and stick them up around the place. On the fridge, by the bed, on your computer, as a bookmark – somewhere where you'll see them often. Try putting some words in context – the 'How much is it?' note, for instance, could go in your wallet.

Building the Picture

We include a chapter on grammar in our books for two main reasons.

Firstly, some people have an aptitude for grammar and find understanding it a key tool to their learning. If you're such a person, then the grammar chapter will help you build a picture of the language, as it works through all the basics.

The second reason for the grammar chapter is that it gives answers to questions you might raise as you hear or memorise some key phrases. You may find a particular word is always used when there is a question – check out the grammar heading on questions and it should explain why. This way you don't have to read the grammar chapter from start to finish, nor do you need to memorise a grammatical point. It will simply present itself to you in the course of your learning. Key grammatical points are repeated throughout the book.

INTRODUCTION

Any Questions?

Try to learn the main question words (see page 40). As you read through different situations, you'll see these words used in the example sentences, and this will help you remember them. So if you want to hire a bicycle, turn to the Bicycles section in Getting Around (use the Contents or Index pages to find it quickly). You've already tried to memorise the word for 'where' and you'll see the word for 'bicycle'. When you come across the sentence 'Where can I hire a bicycle?', you'll recognise the key words and this will help you remember the whole phrase. If there's no category for your need, try the dictionary (the question words are repeated there too, with examples), and memorise the phrases 'Please write that down' and 'How do you say ...?' (page 55).

I've Got a Flat Tyre

Doesn't seem like the phrase you're going to need? Well in fact, it could be very useful. As are all the phrases in this book, provided you have the courage to mix and match them. We have given specific examples within each section. But the key words remain the same even when the situation changes. So while you may not be planning on any cycling during your trip, the first part of the phrase 'I've got ...' could refer to anything else, and there are plenty of words in the dictionary that, we hope, will fit your needs. So whether it's 'a ticket', 'a visa' or 'a condom', you'll be able to put the words together to convey your meaning.

Finally

Don't be concerned if you feel you can't memorise words. On the inside front and back covers are the most essential words and phrases you'll need. You could also try tagging a few pages for other key phrases.

PRONUNCIATION

English-speaking people will find it fairly easy to pronounce Pilipino words as both the vowels and the consonants are pronounced as they are written.

VOWELS
There are five vowels and they have sounds similar to the sounds in the following English words:

a   as the 'a' in 'far'
e   as the 'e' in 'get'
i   as the 'ee' in 'beef'
o   as the 'o' in 'more'
u   as the 'oo' in 'soon'

Diphthongs
The diphthongs, or combinations of vowels, approximate the sounds in the following English words:

ay   as the 'uy' in 'buy'
aw   as the 'ou' in 'mount'
ey   as the 'ay' in 'ray'
iw   produced by making the sound 'ee' and continuing it to 'oo'
oy   as the 'oi' in 'noise'
uy   produced by making the sound 'oo' and continuing it to 'ee'

Vowels in Sequence
If several vowels are written in a sequence, each vowel is pronounced separately.

panauhin (visitor) is pronounced pana-uhin

PRONUNCIATION

CONSONANTS

Most Pilipino consonants are pronounced in the same way as their English counterparts, with the exception of the following:

g   always hard as in 'good', never as in 'gentle'
h   as in 'haste', always aspirated, never silent
r   produced by rolling it to produce a faint trill
s   as in 'sun', never as in 'his'

Consonant Combinations

The only Pilipino consonant which may pose a pronunciation problem is the consonant ng. This sound does occur in English words but in Pilipino it can also occur at the beginning of a word, eg ngayón (now). In a word where ng is followed by a g, both consonants are pronounced separately, eg mang-gá (mango).

ng   as in 'sing'

ASPIRATION

Aspiration is a puff of air which follows a consonant. Pilipino consonants are not aspirated. Compare the aspirated 'p' in 'pin' to the unaspirated 'p' in 'spin'.

STRESS

Stress is the emphasis made by the voice on a particular syllable of a word.

Acute Accent ( )

In a Pilipino word, the stress is marked by the accent sign ( ) on the vowel which is stressed:

masayá   happy

More about Stress

A long word may have one or two stressed syllables:

mátaób   to capsize

The glottal stop is dropped when a suffix is added to the word:

dagâ	mouse/rat
becomes	
dagaín	to become infested with rats

A word with one syllable which comes after a word that is stressed on its last syllable often takes the stress of the previous word:

hindî	no
but	
hindi pô	no, sir/madam

A change in stress can change the meaning of the word:

suka	vomit
sukà	vinegar

GLOTTAL STOP

Some Pilipino vowels are pronounced with what is called a glottal stop. This is done by making the sound of the vowel, then abruptly stopping it, as the 'tt' in the Cockney pronunciation of 'bottle'. A glottal stop is shown by a grave accent (`) or a circumflex (^) on the vowel.

Grave Accent (`)

A word which has the stress on the second-to-last syllable and whose vowel at the end is pronounced with a glottal stop is marked with the grave sign (`):

kandilà	candle

Circumflex (^)

A word, which has the stress on the last syllable and whose vowel at the end of the word is pronounced with a glottal stop following it is marked with the circumflex sign (^):

masamâ	bad

SPELLING CONVENTIONS

Pilipino words are generally pronounced as they are written.
However, there are exceptions such as **ng** (the/of), pronounced
as **nang**, and **mgá** (the, pl), pronounced as **mangá**

The Pilipino alphabet has only 20 letters. The order is the
same except for **k** which comes after **b**. There is a separate entry
for **ng** which comes after **n**

For English-speakers, Pilipino can appear complicated. For instance, you can have a Pilipino sentence with no verb at all, the verb being merely implied, or a sentence that starts with a verb. Root words of nouns, verbs and adjectives can change their meaning with the addition of affixes – prefixes, infixes or suffixes. There are particles that can give a subtle change to the meaning of a sentence. All these quaint differences may make learning Pilipino difficult but also challenging and interesting. This section will attempt to clarify the difficulties with simple explanations and examples.

Please note that the English articles 'the', 'a' and 'an' don't have exact equivalents in Pilipino. Subsequently the Pilipino articles have been shown as the abbreviation *art* in the literal translations.

SENTENCE STRUCTURE
There are two sentence structures in Pilipino.

The Inverted Sentence Structure
You'll find that when talking, most Filipinos use this type of sentence structure. In such a sentence the verb may be absent and merely implied. A sentence can begin with a verb, even if it's not a question. The subject (that which they are talking about) follows. An adjective, an adverb or a noun (which is not the subject) can also begin a sentence.

The river is far. Malayò ang ilog.
  (lit: far the river)

Ray will buy a car. Bíbilí ng awto si Ray.

(lit: will-buy *art* car *art* Ray)

The Regular Sentence Structure

This sentence structure is similar to English. The subject is connected to the predicate by the particle ay. This makes it easy to know which is the subject and which is the predicate (a predicate is a verb, adjective, adverb or noun which relates to the subject), for example in a sentence in which both subject and predicate are nouns. When ay is used by itself in a sentence, it can be roughly translated as certain parts of the English verb 'to be' but when preceding a verb it serves as a helping verb.

The hut is small. Ang kubo ay maliit.

(lit: *art* hut is small)

In a sentence such as the example above, if the word which comes before ay ends in a vowel, the ay can be contracted to y and attached with an apostrophe to the end of that word. The sentence below illustrates this.

The hut is small Ang kubo'y maliít.

The tourists are swimming. Ang mgá turista'y
lumálangóy.

ARTICLES
Articles for Names of People

Unlike English, articles ('the', 'a', 'an') are used with people's names except in the imperative or in direct speech. Different articles are attached to people's names depending on the context:

• When people are the subjects of a sentence

Lorenzo is intelligent.
Si Lorenzo ay matalino.
(lit: *art* Lorenzo is intelligent)

	singular	*plural*
Subject	si	siná
Direct Object	si	siná
Indirect Object	kay	kiná
Indirect Object with prepositions **sa** (to) and **para** (for)	sa; para kay	sa; para kiná
Agent	ni	niná
Possessive	ni	niná

I saw Rafael and Guilliano.
  Nákita ko siná Rafael at Guilliano.
  (lit: were-seen by-me *art* Rafael and Guilliano)

* When people are indirect objects:

  Olivia is reading to Vicky.
  Si Olivia ay nagbábasá kay Vicky.
  (lit: *art* Olivia is reading *art*-to Vicky)

* When people are indirect objects with prepositions:

  Arabella cooked for Priscilla and Diego.
  Naglutò si Arabella para kiná Priscilla at Diego.
  (lit: cooked *art* Arabella for *art* Priscilla and Diego)

* Agent – when people do the action but are not the subject of the sentence. This is similar to the passive indicated with 'by' in English:

  Arnel called Miguel on the telephone.
  Tinagawan ni Miguel si Arnel.
  (lit: was-called-by-telephone *art* Miguel *art* Arnel)

- To indicate possession:

Sandra's dress	barò ni Sandra (lit: dress *art* Sandra)
children of Jose and Tisha	mgá anák niná Jose at Tisha (lit: *art* children *art* Jose and Tisha)

Articles for Common Nouns

Definite articles ('the') and indefinite articles ('a', 'an') aren't exactly the same as in English. However, their rough equivalents are used with common nouns and differ according to context.

Indefinite articles are often not expressed in Pilipino or expressed by the number one (isá).

Peter is a child.	Si Peter ay bata. (lit: *art* Peter is child)
	Si Peter ay isang bata. (lit: *art* Peter is one child)

Definite	singular	plural
Subject	ang	ang mgá
Direct Object	ng	ng mgá
Indirect Object	ang	ang mgá
Indirect Object with prepositions sa (to) and para (for)	sa; para sa	sa mgá; para sa mgá
Agent	ng	ng mgá
Possessive	ng	ng mgá

GRAMMAR

Indefinite		
	singular	plural
Subject	ang; isang	mgá
Direct Object	ng; isang	ng mgá
Indirect Object	ang; ang isang	ang mgá

Indirect Object with
  prepositions sa (to)
  and para (for)
	sa;
	para sa isang
		sa mgá;
		para sa mgá

Agent	ng (isang)	ng mgá
Possessive	ng (isang)	ng mgá

Norma and Guillermo are Filipinos.
> **Mgá Pilipino siná Norma at Guillermo.**
> (lit: *art* Filipinos *art* Norma and Guillermo)

- Common nouns used as subjects:

   The room is clean.
   > **Ang kuwarto ay malinis.**
   > (lit: *art* room is clean)

   The guests are eating.
   > **Kumakain ang mgá panauhin.**
   > (lit: are-eating *art art* guests)

   I received the package.
   > **Tinanggáp ko ang pakete.**
   > (lit: was-received by-me *art* package)

- Common nouns used as direct objects of verbs:

   The tourist bought a souvenir.
   > **Bumilí ng subenir ang turista.**
   > (lit: bought *art* souvenir *art* tourist)

GRAMMAR

She is selling magazines.

> **Nagtitinda siyá ng mgá magasin.**
> (lit: selling she *art art* magazines)

- Common nouns used as indirect objects with prepositions:

I am writing to the embassy.

> **Akó ay sumusulat sa embahada.**
> (lit: I am writing to embassy)

The father is cooking for the children.

> **Naglulutò ang amá para sa mgá batà.**
> (lit: is-cooking *art* father for for *art* children)

- To show possession:

the door of a house

> **ang pintô ng bahay**
> (lit: *art* door of house)

the religion of the Filipinos

> **ang relihiyón ng mgá Pilipino**
> (lit: *art* religion of *art* Pilipinos)

NOUNS

It's very easy to learn Pilipino nouns. They have no gender, and the singular and plural forms are the same. You'll know whether a noun is singular or plural by its article or, if it has none, in the context it is used in the sentence. The fact that Pilipino nouns have no plural forms could be the reason why Filipinos, when speaking in Taglish (Tagalog interspersed with English words), often don't use the plural forms of English nouns, even when they are required.

church	**simbahan**	churches	**mgá simbahan**
the suitcase	**ang maleta**	the suitcases	**ang mgá maleta**

PRONOUNS

'You' in the singular is expressed in Pilipino in two ways, **ikáw** (inf) or **kayó** (pol). When talking with an adult you are familiar with, it is friendlier to use **ikáw**. Otherwise it is always better to use the more formal **kayó**. There is no pronoun 'it' in Pilipino.

There are two forms of 'we' in Pilipino. The pronoun **tayo** includes the person you are talking to, while the pronoun **kamí** excludes that person.

Subject Pronouns

I	akó
you (sg)	ikáw (inf)/kayó (pol)
he/she	siyá
we (includes person spoken to)	tayo
(excludes person spoken to)	kamí
you (pl)	kayó (inf/pol)
they	silá

Alexander and Justine are in the hotel.
  Siná Alexander at Justine ay nasa otél.
  (lit: *art* Alexander and Justine are in hotel)

They are in the hotel.
  Silá ay nasa otél.
  (lit: they are in hotel)

In an inverted sentence structure (see page 19.), the pronoun **ka** is used instead of **ikáw**.

You are going home.   **Ikáw ay uuwî.**
                       (lit: you are going-home)

You are going home.   **Úuwî ka.**
                       (lit: are-going-home you)

GRAMMAR

Direct Object Pronouns

Direct object pronouns don't exist as such in Pilipino – the passive verb sentence structure is used with the agent pronouns to produce a different sentence structure similar to the passive structure commonly used in English.

Agent Pronouns

These pronouns do the action but are not the subject of the sentence, and have the meaning of 'by me', 'by you', 'by her', etc. These are used in the inverted sentence structure (see page 19).

He is using the telephone.

Ginagamit niyá ang teléponó.
(lit: is-being-used by-him *art* telephone)

(by) me	**ko**
(by) you	**mo** (inf)/**ninyó** (pl)
(by) him/her	**niyá**
(by) us	**natin** (inclusive)
	namin (exclusive)
(by) you	**ninyó** (inf/pol)
(by) them	**nilá**

The Pilipino pronoun **kitá** may replace the pronouns **ko** ('by me') and **ikáw** ('you' sg, inf) when used together in a sentence:

I will fetch you.   **Susunduin kitá.**
(lit: will-be-fetched you-by-me)

Susunduin ko ikáw.
(lit: will-be-fetched by-me you)

I like you.   **Gústo kitá.**
(lit: liked you-by-me)

Gústo ko ikáw.
(lit: liked by-me you)

Indirect Object Pronouns

These pronouns have the meaning of 'to me' or 'for me', 'to you' or 'for you', 'to him/her' or 'for him/her' and so on and are mainly used with the prepositions **sa** ('to') and **para sa** ('for', lit: for to).

to/for me	sa/para sa akin
to/for you (sg)	sa/para sa iyó (inf)
	sa/para sa inyó (pol)
to/for him/her	sa/para sa kanyá
to/for us	sa/para sa amin/atin
to you (pl)	sa/para sa inyó (inf/pol)
to/for them	sa/para sa kanilá

We gave coffee to them; We gave them coffee.
Nagbigáy kamí ng kapé sa kanilá.
(lit: gave we *art* coffee to them)

POSSESSION
Possessive Pronouns

These pronouns replace the nouns with possessive adjectives, eg **aking asawa** (my husband) becomes **akin** (mine).

mine	akin
yours (sg)	iyó (inf)/inyó (pol)
his/hers	kanyá
ours	atin/amin
yours (pl)	inyó (inf/pol)
theirs	kanilá

That is mine.   **Iyán ay akin.**
(lit: that is mine)

GRAMMAR

Possessive Adjectives

A possessive adjective is a pronoun that shows possession by a person of something, and therefore comes with a noun. Pilipino possessive adjectives have different forms depending on whether they come before or after the noun:

	Before Noun	After Noun
my	aking	ko
your	iyóng (inf)	mo (inf)
	inyóng (pol)	ninyó (pol)
his/her	kanyáng	niyá
our	ating	natin;
	aming	namin
your	inyóng	ninyó (inf/pol)
their	kaniláng	nilá

This is your umbrella.   **Itó ay iyóng payong.**
(lit: this is your umbrella)

Iyóng payong itó.
(lit: your umbrella this)

VERBS

Pilipino verbs are probably the most complicated and difficult aspect of Pilipino to explain to non-Filipinos.

Verb Conjugation & Tenses

The infinitive form of the Pilipino verb is made up of the root of the verb and an affix. An affix is added to the beginning, middle or end of a verb in order to change its meaning and use in a sentence.

GRAMMAR

A verb is conjugated according to the affix and verbs are grouped accordingly. Changing the affix on the root of a verb will give it another meaning altogether:

kain   'consumption of food by eating'

with the affix *um*

ku*m*ain	to eat
I ate a fish.	**Kumain akó ng isdá.**
	(lit: ate I *art* fish)

with the affix *in*

ki*n*ain	to eat (to be eaten by)
I was eaten by a fish.	**Kinain ako ng isda.**
	(lit: was-eaten I *art* fish)

One simple thing, however, about Pilipino verbs is that they have no conjugation endings. This means that the verb remains unchanged with different pronouns, and from singular to plural. For example:

I am leaving	**umáalís akó**
	(lit: am-leaving I)
you are leaving	**umáalís ka**
	(lit: are-leaving you)
he/she is leaving	**umáalís siyá**
	(lit: is-leaving he/she)

Conjugations

Pilipino verbs are split into two major groups: the active and the passive. These are indicated by affixes and the most common are shown below. The affixes also change the verb roots into infinitives.

GRAMMAR

Active

mag-	ma-	maka-	um-	-um-

bayad	pay (verb root)
*mag*bayad	to pay
alís	leave (verb root)
*um*alís	to leave
bili	buy (verb root)
b*um*ili	to buy

Passive

-in/-hin	-ma	paki-	i-	-an/-han	pa-in

basa	read (verb root)
basá*hin*	to read (to be read by)
sulat	write
*i*sulat	to write (to be written)
tawag	call by phone (verb root)
tawag*an*	to call by phone

Tenses

Tenses in Pilipino are formed by a complicated combination of affixes and repeated syllables. It's really beyond the scope of this phrasebook to give a detailed description of the way tenses are formed but some examples are shown below.

to go away (from somewhere)	**umalís**
Present	**umáalís**
Past	**umalís**
Future	**áalís**
to buy	**bumilí**
Present	**bumíbilí**
Past	**bumilí**
Future	**bíbilí**
to go home	**umuwî**
Present	**umúuwî**
Past	**umuwî**
Future	**úuwî**
to feel warm	**mainítan**
Present	**naíinitan**
Past	**nainitan**
Future	**maíinitan**

GRAMMAR

Imperative

The request or command forms of verbs are the same as the infinitive. You start a request or a command with the verb. Using the polite particle **ngâ** when making a request will make it sound more gracious.

Please speak.	**Magsalitâ ka ngâ.**
	(lit: speak you particle)

Another way of expressing a request is by adding the prefix **pakí-** to the root of the verb.

Please pass the salt.	**Pakiabót mo ngâ ang asín.**
	(lit: prefix-pass by-you particle *art* salt)

KEY VERBS

to arrive	dumatíng
to be	(see page 33.)
to become	magíng
to bring	dalhín
to buy	bumilí
to come (closer)	lumapit
to depart/leave	umalís
to drink	uminóm
to eat	kumain
to be eaten	kainin
to give	magbigáy
to go	magpatuloy
to have	magkaroón (see page 34.)
to know	málaman
to live (life)	mabuhay
to live (somewhere)	manirahan
to love	umibig
to make	gumawâ
to meet	magtagpô
to need	mangailangan
to return	magbalík
to say	magsabi
to stay (remain)	mátirá
to stay (somewhere)	tumirá
to take	kunin
to understand	maintidihan
to want/like	magustohan

TO BE

The verb 'to be' has no exact Pilipino equivalent. As mentioned under the heading Sentence Structures, the particle ay can be roughly translated as a form of the verb 'to be'.

Roberto and Elsie are doctors.
> **Siná Roberto at Elsie ay mgá doktór.**
> (lit: *art* Roberto and Elsie are *art* doctors)

When ay comes before a verb, it serves as what is commonly known as a 'helping verb'.

Lina is teaching Pilipino.
> **Si Lina ay nagtuturò ng Pilipino.**
> (lit: *art* Lina is teaching *art* Pilipino)

TO HAVE

The state of having or owning is expressed by mayroon (sometimes meron) or may (commonly pronounced mey). It must be stressed though that mayroon and may are not verbs – they are a type of possessive particle.

Do you have a visa?
> **Mayroón ba kayóng bisa?**
> (lit: have particle you visa)

They have a house in Antipolo.
> **Mayroón siláng bahay sa Antipolo.**
> (lit: have they house in Antipolo)

May is used only when followed by a noun, which loses its article if it is in the singular form.

I have a relative in Cubao.
> **May kamág-anak ako sa Cubao.**
> (lit: have relative I in Cubao)

The verb **magkaroón** is another form of 'to have' and has the following tense forms:

Present	have	**nagkákaroón**
Past	had	**nagkaroón**
Future	will have	**magkákaroón**

Alternatively, you can make it simpler for yourself by just adding the prefix **magka-** to the noun to be possessed. The new word is treated like a verb and therefore has verb forms. Consider the following:

'to have a problem'		**magkaproblema**
Present	have a problem	**nagkakaproblema**
Past	had a problem	**nagkaproblema**
Future	will have a problem	**magkakaproblema**

There Is or There Are

May can also mean 'there is' or 'there are':

> There is a dance next door.
> **May sayawan sa kapitbahay.**
> (lit: there-is dance in next-door)

> There was a fire in Quezon City yesterday.
> **May sunog sa Quezon City kahapon.**
> (lit: there-was fire in Quezon City yesterday)

ADJECTIVES
Position of Adjectives in a Sentence

Adjectives in Pilipino can come before or after the words they describe.

An adjective ending with a vowel which comes before a noun is given an **-ng** ending. If it ends with a consonant, the particle **na** comes between the adjective and the noun.

sweet-smelling flower	**mabangóng bulaklák**
	(lit: sweet-smelling-ng flower)
	bulaklák na mabangó
	(lit: flower particle sweet-smelling)

On the other hand, if the adjective ending with a vowel comes after the noun it is describing, the noun, not the adjective, gets the **-ng** ending.

happy person	**táong masayá**
	(lit: person-ng happy)

If the noun being described ends with a consonant, the particle **na** comes between the noun and the adjective.

cold water	**tubig na malamíg**
	(lit: water particle cold)

Comparatives

To say that a 'person is more ... than another person', **mas/lalo** ('more') is put before the adjective and **kaysa kay** (sg)/**kaysa kina** (pl) before the name of the person to whom that person is being compared. **Mas** is more commonly used and is actually the Spanish word for 'more'. The ending **-ng** is attached to **lalo** to make pronunciation easy.

Mel is more handsome than Jason.
   Mas/Lalong guwapo si Mel kaysa kay Jason.
   (lit: more handsome *art* Mel than *art* Jason)

Susan is taller than Constance and Marcia.
   Mas/Lalong mataás si Susan kaysa kina Constance at Marcia.
   (lit: more tall *art* Susan than *art* Constance)

To compare nouns or names of places or things, **mas/lalo** (more) is put before the adjective, then **kaysa sa** (sg) or **sa mgá** (pl) goes next to the thing being compared.

Australia is bigger than the Philippines.
> **Mas/Lalong malakí ang Australya kaysa sa Pilipinas.**
> (lit: more big *art* Australia than *art* Philippines)

The hotel is taller than the houses.
> **Ang otél ay mas/lalong mataás kaysa sa mgá bahay.**
> (lit: *art* hotel is more tall than *art art* houses)

To say that 'someone or something is as .. as ...', **kasing** is attached to the describing word.

Trina is as pretty as Wendy.
> **Si Trina ay kásingganda ni Wendy.**
> (lit: *art* Trina is as-pretty-as *art* Wendy)

Superlatives

To say that someone or something is 'the most ... ', **pinaka** is attached to the adjective.

The coldest season is winter.
> **Ang pinakamalamig na panahón ay ang taglamíg.**
> (lit: *art* coldest particle weather is *art* winter)

He is the laziest.
> **Pinakatamád siyá.**
> (lit: laziest he)

More About Adjectives

To say 'that someone or something is very ...' you simply repeat the adjective, with the linking particle **na** between the two adjectives

very expensive
> **mahál na mahál**
> (lit: expensive particle expensive)

If the adjective ends with a vowel, -ng is attached to the end of
the first adjective and a hyphen comes between the two adjectives.

very cheap   **murang-mura**
                    (lit: cheap-particle cheap)

Or you attach **nápaka** to the adjective.

very fast   **nápakabilís**
                    (lit: particle-fast)

COMMON ADJECTIVES

pretty/beautiful	magandá
ugly	pangit
expensive	mahál
cheap	mura
big	malakí
small	maliít
heavy	mabigát
light (in weight)	magaáng
rich	mayaman
poor/difficult	mahirap
clean	malinis
dirty	madumí
right	tamà
wrong	malî
sweet	matamís
sour	maasim
far	malayò
noisy	maingay
quite	tahimik

GRAMMAR

ADVERBS
Adverbs describe verbs, adjectives or other adverbs.

Position of Adverbs
Adverbs may come at any part of the sentence. Consider the following examples. The adverb is **mabilís** (quickly).

She ran quickly.	**Mabilís siyáng tumakbó.** (lit: quickly she ran)
	Siyá ay tumakbó nang mabilís. (lit: she particle ran particle quickly)

Some words can be interchangeably used as adjectives or adverbs without changing their forms.

slow train	**mabagal na tren** (lit: slow particle train)
	tren na mabagal (lit: train particle slow)
walk slowly	**mabagal na lumakad** (lit: slowly particle walk)
	lumakad nang mabagal (lit: walk particle slowly)

Adverbs of Manner
These adverbs describe how an action is done.

quickly/fast	**mabilís**
loudly	**malakás**
slowly	**dahan-dahan**
softly	**mahinà**

swiftly	matulin
clearly	malinaw
carefully	maingat
like this/in this manner	ganitó
like that/in that manner	ganyán/ganoón

Adverbs of Place

These adverbs of place are used when, in a subject-predicate sentence structure, **ay** acts as the verb or in an inverted sentence structure in which there is no verb. They answer the question: **nasaan?** (where?).

here	nandito
there	nándiyán/nándoón
up/above	nasa itaás
down/below	nasa ibabá
in front	nasa harapán
at the back	nasa likurán
inside	nasa loób
outside	nasa labás

These adverbs of place are used when there is a verb in the sentence and answer the question: **saán** (where?).

here	dito
there	diyán/doón
up/above	sa itaás
down/below	sa ibabâ
in front	sa harapán
at the back	sa likurán
inside	sa loób
outside	sa labás

GRAMMAR

QUESTIONS

Questions are asked with a slight rise in intonation at the end of the sentence.

'Yes' or 'No' Questions

You can ask questions using either the regular sentence structure or the inverted sentence structure (see page 19). To make it clear that you are asking something and not stating it, use the particle ba Ba should come after the subject in a regular sentence structure and after the predicate in the inverted sentence structure.

> Josie is in the Philippines.
>> Si Josie ba ay nasa Pilipinas?
>> (lit: *art* Josie Particle in Phillipines)
>>
>> Nasa Pilipinas ba si Josie?
>> (lit: in Philippines particle *art* Josie)

Questions with Interrogative Pronouns

A question may be introduced by an interrogative pronoun.

who	sino
what	anó
when	kailán
where	saán/nasaán
how	paano
why	bakit
how many	ilán
how much (price)	magkano
whose	kanino

Some examples of questions with interrogative pronouns

Who is the manager?	**Sino ba ang manedyer?**
	(lit: who particle *art* manager)
What is that?	**Ano ba iyán?**
	(lit: what particle that)
When is he coming?	**Kailán siya darating?**
	(lit: when he-is coming)
Where do you live?	**Saán ba kayó nakatirá?**
	(lit: where particle you live)
How much is the book?	**Magkano ba ang libró?**
	(lit: how-much particle *art* book)

NEGATIVES
No

The answer 'no' is **hindî**

Is he Filipino? – No.
Pilipino ba siyá? – **Hindî.**
(lit: Filipino particle he – no)

However, a question with **mayroón** or **may** is answered negatively with **wala**.

Do you have a problem? – No.
May problema ka ba? – **Walâ.**
(lit: have problem you particle – no)

Non-Pilipino speakers generally make the mistake of answering with **hindî**, the word for 'no'.

To negate the subject or predicate, whether it is a word or a phrase, you put '**hindî**' before the word or phrase negated.

GRAMMAR

Ricardo is not a lawyer.   **Hindî abogado si Ricardo.**
(lit: not lawyer *art* Ricardo)

To negate the imperative, **huwág** is used and has the meaning 'don't'.

Don't drink.   **Huwág kang uminóm.**
(lit: do-not you drink)

MODALS

Modal verbs are known as 'helping verbs' and are used together with the infinitive form of the main verb.

Obligations: Must/Have to/Need to

You should use **dapat** or **kailangan** to say: 'I have to/need to do something'.

I have to wait.   **Dapat akóng maghintáy.**
(lit: must I to-wait)

We need to find a room.   **Kailangan tayong humanap ng kuwarto.**
(lit: need we-particle to-find *art* room)

To Want/Like To

- You use **gústo** if you want to say 'I like/want to do something.' Gústo – which can be either a noun or an adjective but isn't a verb – is used to express the desire to or the liking to do something.

    Do you want to learn Pilipino?
        Gústo mo bang matuto ng Pilipino?
        (lit: desire your particle to-learn *art* Pilipino)

- **Gústo** may also be used by itself, in which case, it takes the meaning of liking something or someone.

Joey and Chris like mangoes.

Gústo nilá ng manggá.
(lit: liking of Joey and Chris *art* mangoes)

I like Gina.

Gústo ko si Gina.
(lit: liking my *art* Gina)

- You can use another helping verb, **ayaw**, to express not to like/ want to do something.

    He doesn't want to travel.

    Ayaw niyáng maglakbay.
    (lit: dislike his to-travel)

    Hindi niya gústong maglakbay.
    (lit: not his liking to-travel)

Can/To Be Able to

- You use **maáarì** or **puwede** if you want to say 'I can/am able' to do something'.

    Can we get on the bus?

    Máaarì ba kamíng sumakáy sa bus?
    (lit: can particle we-particle to-get on bus)

    Can you ring me?

    Puwede mo ba akóng tawagan?
    (lit: can by-you particle I-particle be-called)

- A simpler way to express 'can/to be able to' is attaching the prefix **ma** to the verb.

    Can you fetch me?

    Masusundô mo ba akó?
    (lit: can-be-fetched by-you particle I)

If you want to say 'I know how to do something', use **alám**

Aly knows how to dance the tango.
Alám ni Aly magsayáw ng tango.
(lit: knowledge of Aly to-dance *art* tango)

PREPOSITIONS

In the prepositions given below the preposition **sa** is the counterpart of many English prepositions. It's also often used in combination with other prepositions.

in December	sa Disyembre
in San Juan	sa San Juan
at noon	sa tanghalì
at home	sa bahay
on Wednesday	sa Miyérkolés
on the roof	sa bubóng
against racism	laban sa rasismo
toward Bulacán	patungò sa Bulacán
from Pangasinán	buhat/mulâ sa Pangasinán
about her	tungkól sa kanyá
in front of the restaurant	sa haráp ng restaurán
inside the car	sa loób ng awto
of	ng
across the river	sa kabilâ ng ilog
for us	para sa amin/atin

CONJUNCTIONS

because	dahil/sapagká't
but	pero/nguni't
and	at
while	habang/samantalâ
if	kung

or	ó
even if/though	kahit
when	noóng (past)/kapág (future)
consequently	kayâ
so that	nang

Some sentences using Pilipino conjunctions:

We'll go to the carnival if you'll come along.
    Púpuntá kamí sa karnabál kung sasama ka.
    (lit: will-go we to carnival if will-go you)

Do I sign here or there?
    Pípirmá ba akó dito ó diyán?
    (lit: sign particle I here or there)

The passport and the money are in the bag.
    Ang pasport at ang pera ay nasa supot.
    (lit: *art* passport and *art* money are in bag)

I'm leaving even if it is raining.
    Áalís akó kahit umúulán.
    (lit: am-leaving I even-if raining)

MAKING YOUR OWN SENTENCES

Now that you've gone through the grammar, try out what you have learned by translating the sentences below into Pilipino. Cover the translation opposite the English sentences and try and work them out yourself. Have fun!

I am Juan.	Akó si Juan.
	Si Juan akó.
The hotel is clean.	Malinis ang otél.
	Ang otél ay malinis.

That is mine.	Akin iyán./Iyán ay akin.
They are eating. (kumain)	Kumakain sila.
	Silá ay kumakain.
Are you a tourist? (inf)	Turísta ka bá?
	Ikáw ba ay turista?
Be happy!	Magíng masayá ka!
Is she here?	Nandito ba siyá?
	Siyá ba ay nandito?
We are in Baguio.	Nasa Baguio kamí.
	Kamí ay nasa Baguio.
Richie is richer than Bobby.	Mas mayaman si Richie kaysa kay Bobby.
	Si Richie ay mas mayaman kaysa kay Bobby.
How many are you?	Ilán ba kayó?
	Kayó ba ay ilán?
Why is it hot here?	Bakit mainit dito?
This is my car.	Awto ko itó.
	Aking awto itó.
	Itó ay awto ko.
	Itó ay aking awto.

MEETING PEOPLE

YOU SHOULD KNOW

It's easy to strike up a conversation with Filipinos, especially if you know some Pilipino, although you'll probably find that many understand and speak English to a varying degree. The people outside the cities and in the provinces are generally shy but, once they overcome their shyness, they are as friendly and accomodating, if not more so, to strangers, as their city counterparts. You will be regarded well if, when speaking to adults you don't know well, older people or people of status, you use the polite forms of speech.

Yes.	Ohò/Opò. (pol)
	Oo. (inf)
No.	Hindi hô. (pol)
	Hindî. (inf)
Excuse me.	Mawaláng-galang na nga hô. (pol)
	Mawaláng-galang. (inf)
What did you say?	Anó hô?
Hello.	Kumusta hô.
Bye.	Sige na muna. (inf)
Thank you.	Salámat hô.
Many thanks.	Maráming salámat hô.

GREETINGS & GOODBYES

Filipinos in the provinces, particularly the older ones, are in general very polite to strangers. Here are some useful phrases.

Good morning.	Magandáng umaga hô. (pol)
	Magandáng umaga. (inf)
Good morning to you too.	Magandáng umaga namán hô.
Good day (noon).	Magandáng tanghali hô.
Good afternoon.	Magandáng hapon hô. (pol)
	Magandáng hapon. (inf)

| Good evening. | Magandáng gabí hô. |
| Goodbye. | Paalam na hô. |

Civilities

Filipinos are generous and if you see Filipinos eating something, more likely than not they will offer you what they're eating or a piece of it. It's quite alright to refuse, but it's friendlier to have even a small token piece. On the other hand, when offered something, Filipinos will more likely graciously refuse, but that doesn't mean that they will refuse altogether. Make the offer once again and they will probably accept the offer this time. 'Thank you' is not used as much in Pilipino as it is in English. Saying 'Thank you' for a service you would expect may sound superfluous.

Thank you (very much).	(Maraming) salamat hô. (pol)
	Maraming salamat. (inf)
You're welcome.	Walá hong anumán. (pol)
	(lit: none particle anything)
	Waláng anumán. (inf)
Excuse me/Sorry.	Iskyús/Sori hô.
May I/Do you mind?	Puwede hô ba?

Forms of Address

You can use the common forms of address in English – 'Mr, Miss, Ms, Mrs, Dr, etc'. When addressing people of status or older people the particle pô/hô may be used together with the pronoun kayó ('you'). You can leave out these particles too. Don't worry, that won't make you less polite.

| How are you? | Kumusta hô kayó? |

Use the title mamà for a man who is a stranger or ale for a woman.

| How much are the atis? | Magkano hô ba ang atis, mamà? |

| How much is a kilogram of mangoes? | Magkano hô ba ang kilo ng manggá, ale? |

You may also use misis, or mis (Mrs., or Miss) for adult female strangers.

| Do I sign here? | Dito hô ba akó pipirma, mis? |
| We are leaving. | Áalís na hô kamí, misis. |

Use 'sir' for a professional man or 'ma'am' for a professional woman:

| Here is my passport. | Eto hô ang pasport ko, sir. |
| When are my papers coming? | Kelan hô ba dáratíng ang mgá papeles ko, ma'am? |

The more friendly and familiar term páre (for a man) or brad (for a younger adult, if you are yourself one) may also be used for a man who is a stranger:

| Excuse me, my friend. | Iskyús lang, pare. (inf) |
| Where's the nearest bus stop? | Násaán ba ang pinakamalapit na hintuan ng bus, brad? (inf) |

BODY LANGUAGE

Most Filipinos signify 'Yes' by raising the eyebrows or lifting the head upwards slightly. They also do this when they greet friends.

You can hiss to gain attention, for example, when calling a waiter in a restaurant. When you want to pay the bill, make the figure of a rectangle in the air with your index finger and thumb.

It's considered impolite to pass between people conversing or facing one another. If you must do so, the Filipino polite way is to extend an arm or two arms with the hands clasped and pointing downwards either without saying anything or murmuring iskyús

Touching, especially women, is not taken well by Filipinos. You'll notice that a Filipino man will extend his hand to shake yours but a Filipino woman will not readily do so. When being introduced to a couple or greeting them, you shake hands with the man and smile with a nod of the head to the woman.

FIRST ENCOUNTERS

It's better to use the polite form for adults you don't know well. When you use the formal form with friends or younger adults, you'll more likely get the comment: 'Don't use hô/pô with me. I'm not that old yet'.

How are you?	Kumustá hô kayó? (pol)
Hi (Bong), how are you?	Hoy (Bong), kumustá ka? (inf)
Fine. And you?	Mabuti namán. Ikáw? (inf)
So-so.	Eto.
What's your name?	Anóng pangalan ninyó? (pol)
	Anóng pangalan mo? (inf)
What's his/her name?	Anóng pangalan niyá? (inf)
My name is ...	Akó si ...
I'd like to introduce you to ...	Gusto ko hô kayóng ipakilala kay ... (pol)
	Gusto kitáng ipakilala kay ... (inf)
I'm pleased to meet you.	Ikinagágalák ko kayóng makilala. (pol)
	Ikinagágalák kitáng makilala. (inf)

MAKING CONVERSATION

Do you live here?	Dito ba kayó nakatirá? (pol)
	Dito ka ba nakatirá (inf)
Are you from here?	Tagá-dito ba kayó? (pol)
	Tagá-dito ka ba? (inf)
Where are you going?	Saán kayó púpuntá? (pol)
	Saán ka púpúnta? (inf)
What are you doing?	Ano hô ang ginágawâ ninyó? (pol)
	Anóng ginágawâ mo? (inf)
What do you think (about ...)?	Ano hô ang palagáy ninyó (sa ...)? (pol)
	Anóng palagáy mo (sa ...)? (inf)
Can I take a photo (of you)?	Máarì ko ba kayóng kunan ng litrato? (pol)
	Máaarì ba kitáng kúnan ng litrato? (inf)
What's this called?	Anó ho báng tawag dito?
Beautiful, isn't it!	Ang gandá namán, di ba? (inf)
It's very nice here.	Nápakagandá hô dito.
We love it here.	Nagúgustuhán hô namin dito.
What a cute baby!	Ang kyút ng beybi!
Are you waiting too?	Naghíhintáy din ba kayó?(pol)
	Naghíhintáy ka din ba? (inf)
That's strange!	Nakapagtátaká yón! (inf)
That's funny (amusing)	Nakákatawá yón! (inf)

DID YOU KNOW ... You don't have to be punctual as it's very normal, in fact expected, to turn up 30 minutes late. It's also common to take your shoes off before entering someone's home in the country.

Are you here on holiday?	Naparito ba kayó para magbakasyón? (pol)
	Naparito ka bá para magbakasyón? (inf)
I'm here ...	Naparito hô akó para ... (pol)
for a holiday	magbakasyón
on business	magnegosyo
to study	mag-aral
How long are you here for?	Gaáno katagál kayó dito? (pol)
	Gaáno katagál ka dito? (inf)
I'm/We're here for ...	Tátagál hô akó/kamí dito nang ...
weeks/days.	na linggó/araw.
Do you like it here?	Nagugustuhán ba niyó dito? (pol)
	Nagugustuhán mo bá dito? (inf)
I/We like it here very much.	Gustóng-gustó ko/namin hô dito. (pol)
	Gustóng-gustó ko/namin dito. (inf)

USEFUL PHRASES

Sure.	Sigurado, hô.
Just a minute.	Teka muna hô.
It's OK.	OK/Ayos lang.
It's important.	Importante hô yón.
It's not important.	Hindi hô importante yón.
It's possible.	Posible hô yón.
It's not possible.	Hindí hô posible yón.
Look!	Tignán hô niyó!
I'm ready.	Handâ na hô akó.
Are you ready?	Handâ na bá kayó? (pol)
	Handâ ka na bá? (inf)
Good luck!	Suwértihín sana kayó! (pol)
	Suwértihín sana ikáw! (inf)

MEETING PEOPLE

Just a second!	Saglít lang hô! (pol)
	Saglít lang! (inf)
Maybe.	Baká hô.
Never mind.	Hindi hô bale.
I don't know.	Ewan ko hô.
Correct.	Tama hô.
It's up to you.	Kayo náng bahalà.
Let's go!	Tayo na hô! (pol)
	Tayo ná! (inf)
Where are you off to?	Saán hô ang lakad niyó? (pol)
	Saán ang lakad mo? (inf)

NATIONALITIES

Most Filipinos know the names of major countries, cities and continents, as well as the nationalities, in English.

Where are you from?	Tagasaán hô kayó? (pol)
	Tagasaán ka? (inf)
I'm from ...	Tagá ... hô akó. (pol)
Australia	Australya
Africa	Áprika
Europe	Yurópa
Asia	Asya

America	Amériká
Japan	Hapón
the Philippines	Pilipinas
the USA	Istéyts (Amériká)
Canada	Kánada

I live in ...	Sa ... hô akó nakatirá.
the city	siyudád
the countryside	kabukiran
the mountains	kabundukan
the seaside	tabíng-dagat
the suburbs of ...	labás ng lunsód ng ...
a village	baryo

CULTURAL DIFFERENCES

How do you do this in your country?	Paáno niyóng ginágawâ itó sa bayan niyó?
Is this a local or national custom?	Kaugalian hô ba itó dito sa lugár niyó o sa buóng bayan?
I don't want to offend you.	Ayokong ko hong saktán ang damdamin niyó.
I'm sorry, it's not the custom in my country.	Sori, pero hindi hô iyán kaugalian sa bayan namin.
I'm not accustomed to this.	Hindi hô akó sanáy sa ganyán.
I don't mind watching, but I'd prefer not to participate.	Mas gustó ko hong manoód kaysa sumali.
That's not allowed in our country.	Bawal hô iyán sa aming bayan.
Go ahead. I'll just watch.	Sige hô. Manónoód na lang hô akó.

AGE

Filipinos don't mind being asked their age, so it would not be unusual for them to ask yours.

How old ...?	Iláng taón ...?
are you (to a child)	ka ná
are you (to an adult)	na hô kayó
is your son/daughter	na hô ang anák niyó

| I'm ... years old. | ... ng taón na hô akó. |

See Numbers, page 151, for your age.

LANGUAGE DIFFICULTIES

Although most Filipinos speak English and Pilipino, accent differences in the different regions may make it difficult for you to understand some of them.

Do you speak English?	Marunong ba kayóng mag-Inglés?
Yes, I do.	Oo, marunong akó.
No, I don't.	Hindi hô akó marunong.
Does anyone speak English?	Meron hô bang marunong mag-Inglés dito?
I speak a little.	Marunong hô akó nang kauntì.
Do you understand?	Náiintindihán ba ninyó?
I understand.	Naiintindihán ko hô.
I don't understand.	Hindî ko hô náiintindihán.
Could you speak more slowly?	Puwede niyó bang bagalan ang pagsalitâ niyó?
Could you repeat that?	Pakíulit niyó ngâ yón.
Please write it down.	Pakísulat niyó ngâ yón.
How do you say ...?	Papáno ho ba sabíhin ...?
What does ... mean?	Ano hô ang ibig sabihin ng ...?

OCCUPATIONS

What (work) do you do?	Anóng trabaho niyó? (pol)

I am a/an ...	... hô akó
architect	arkitekto
artist	pintór
businessperson	mangangalakal
	komersyánte
carpenter	karpintero
doctor	doktór (m)/doktora (f)
electrician	elektrisista
engineer	inhinyero
farmer	magsasaka
journalist	peryodista
lawyer	abogado/a (m/f)
mechanic	mekánikó
nurse	nars
office worker	empleado/a (m/f)
plumber	tubero
scientist	sáyantist
student	istudyánte
teacher	títser/gurò
waiter	weyter (m)/weytres (f)
writer	mánunulát

I'm unemployed.	Walá akóng trabaho. (inf)
What are you studying?	Ano báng pinágaaralan mo? (inf)
I'm studying ...	... hô ang pinágaaralan ko. (pol)
art	ang sining
arts/humanities	sining/humanities
business	pangangalakal
engineering	inhiniyeriya
languages	mga wikà
law	abogasiya

medicine	medisina
Pilipino	Pilipino
science	aghám
teaching	pagtuturò

FEELINGS

I'm ...	... hô ako. (pol)
happy	masayá
sad	malungkót
embarassed	nahíhiyâ
angry	galít
annoyed	inís
bored	yamót
tired	pagód
sleepy	antók
hungry	gutóm
thirsty	uháw

OPINIONS

Do you like going to the ...?	Mahilig ba kayóng pumuntá sa ...? (pol)
	Mahilig ka bang pumuntá sa ...? (inf)
cinema	sinehán
concert	konsiyérto
disco	disko
theatre	teatro

I like ...	Mahilig hô akóng ... (pol)
	Mahilig akóng ... (inf)
travelling	maglakbay
reading	magbasá
watching TV	manoód ng TV

gardening	maghardín
visiting friends	magbisita ng mgá kaibigan
to swim	lumangóy
cooking	maglutò
collecting things	mangulekta ng mgá bagay-bagay
Are you interested in ...?	Interesado ba kayó sa ...? (pol)
	Interesado ka ba sa ...? (inf)
politics	pulítiká
sports	ispórt
cars	mgá awto
fashion	moda
animals	mgá hayop

FINDING YOUR WAY

Most of the signs in the airport and train stations are in English, so you won't encounter any problems getting around.

Excuse me, can I ask you something?	Iskyús hô, puwede ho bang magtanóng?
Where's the ...?	Násaán hô ang ...?
bus station	terminál ng bus
train station	istasyón ng tren
road to (Bontoc)	daán papuntáng (Bontoc)
nearest LRT station	pinakamalapit na istasyón ng LRT
Metro station	istasyón ng MetroTren
What time does the ... leave/ arrive?	Anóng oras hô áalís/dáratíng ang ...?
aeroplane	eropláno
boat	bapór
bus	bus
train	tren
What ... is this?	Ano hô bang ... itó?
street	kalye
city	siyudád
village	baryo
province	probinsya
town	bayan
How do we get to ...?	Papano hô namin maráratíng ang ...?
Is it far from/near here?	Malayò/malapit hô ba dito?
Are there other means of getting there?	Meron hô pa bang ibáng paraán pumuntá doón? (pol)

GETTING AROUND

| Can we walk there? | Puwede ho bang lakarin? |
| Can you show me on the map? | Puwede ho ba niyóng ipakita sa mapa? (pol) |

DIRECTIONS

Turn at the ...	Likó hô sa ...
next corner	súsunod na kánto
traffic lights	ílaw

Straight ahead.	Tulóy-tulóy lang hô.
To the right.	Kanan hô/lang. (pol/inf)
To the left.	Kaliwá hô.(pol)
	Kaliwâ lang.(inf)

behind ...	sa likód ng ...
in front of ...	sa haráp ng ...
far	malayò
near	malapit
opposite	katapát ng
north	norte/hilagà
south	sud/timog
east	silangan
west	kanluran

Cross the road ...	Tumawíd kayó sa
at the next corner	súsunód na kanto
at the traffic lights	ilaw
at the roundabout	rotonda

ADDRESSES

Addresses are written this way:

> 95 Pedro Tuazon Blvd., Cubao, Quezon City.

The house number is 95, the street is Pedro Tuazon Blvd., the suburb is Cubao and the city is Quezon City.

BUYING TICKETS

Where can I buy a ticket?	Saán hô maaring bumilí ng tiket?
We want to go to ...	Gústo hô naming pumuntá sa ...
Can you show us on the map, please?	Máaarì niyó bang ipakita sa amin sa mapa?
Do I need to book?	Kailangan ho bang magreserba ng lugár?
I'd like to book a seat to ...	Gústo ko hong magreserba ng úpuan papuntáng ...
It's full.	Punô na hô.
Can I get a stand-by ticket?	Makakakuha hô kayâ akó ng stand-by tiket?
I'd like ...	... nga hô.
a one-way ticket	isáng one-way tiket.
a return ticket	isáng round trip tiket; isáng bálikang tiket
two tickets	dalawáng tiket
a student's fare	isáng tiket para sa istudyante
a child's fare	isáng tiket para sa batà
1st/2nd class	primera/segunda klase

AIR

Is there a flight to (Ormoc)?	May flight hô bang papuntáng (Ormoc)?
When's the next flight to (Cebu)?	Kelan hô ang súsunód na flight papuntáng (Cebú)?
How long does the flight take?	Gaano hô katagál ang flight?
What's the flight number?	Ano hô ang número ng flight?
What time do I have to check in at the airport?	Anóng oras hô akó dapat mag-check in sa airport?
Is there a bus to the airport?	Meron hô bang bus papuntáng airport?
Where's the baggage claim?	Saán ko hô kukunin ang aking bagahe?
What's the charge for excess luggage?	Magkano hô ang singíl sa bawat kilo na sobra?
I'd like to ... my reservation.	Gústo ko hóng ... ang aking reservation.
cancel	kanselahín
change	bagúhin
confirm	tiyakín

At Customs

I have nothing to declare.	Walá hô akóng iúulat.
I have something to declare.	Meron hô akóng iúulat.
Do I have to declare this?	Kailangan ko hô bang iulat itó?
This is all my luggage.	Yan na hô lahát ang bagahe ko.
I didn't know I had to declare it.	Hindî ko hô alám na kailangan kong iyulat yan.
May I call our embassy/ consulate?	Máaarì ko hô bang tawagan ang aming embahada/ konsulado?

BUS

Regular buses and air-conditioned buses ply the Manila area. If you want a comfortable ride, take the air-conditioned bus which, of course, costs more. When you want to get off a regular bus, you say Para! (Stop!) loudly. There are designated bus stops, but you can get off anywhere you like, depending on the mood of the driver and the traffic situation. It's always good to have the exact fare ready when you get on the bus otherwise, the conductor might forget to give back your change.

An alternative to buses are jeepneys, which are converted US army jeeps left over from the second world war. A jeepney ride, although uncomfortable because passengers are cramped in , is an experience worth going through, not only because of the colourfulness of the vehicle, but also because of the clever way the jeepney weaves in and out of traffic without getting into an accident.

Where's the bus stop?	Násaán hô ang hintuan ng bus?
Which bus goes to ...?	Alíng bus hô ang papuntá sa ...?
Does this bus go to ...?	Papuntá hô ba itóng bus na itó sa ...?
How often do buses come?	Gaanó hô kadalás dumáraán ang mgá bus?
What time is the ... bus?	Anóng óras hô dáratíng ang ... bus?
next	súsunód na
first	unang
last	hulíng
Could you let me know when we get to ...?	Puwede ho báng sabihin ninyó sa akin kung nasa ... na tayo?

GETTING AROUND

Where do I get the bus for ...?	Saán hô akó kukuha ng bus papuntáng ...?
My change, please.	Ang suklí ko hô.
Sorry, I don't have loose change.	Sori hô, walâ akóng barya.

TRAIN

Traffic in metropolitan Manila is a problem so the best way to get around is to take the LRT (Light Rail Transit) which goes from Bulacan to Caloocan City. It's a fast way to get anywhere but it's not the most comfortable way. If you want to go farther south, take the Metro Tren which goes from Tutuban Station to Laguna.

What station is this?	Ano hóng istasyón itó?
What's the next station?	Anó hô ba ang súsunód na istasyón?
Does this train stop at ...?	Humíhintô ho ba ang tren na itó sa ...?
The train is delayed/cancelled.	Náhulí/Nákanselá hô ang tren.
How long will it be delayed?	Gaanó katagál hô mahúhulí?

DID YOU KNOW ... There are over seven thousand islands in the Philippine archipelago so even if you only spent a day on each it would take you over 20 years to set foot on each one.

TAXI

Is this taxi free?	Bakánte hô bang taksing itó?
Please take me to ...	Dalhín nga niyó akó sa ...
How much does it cost to go to ...?	Magkano hô papuntáng ...?
How much is the fare?	Magkano hô ang pamasahe?
Do we pay extra for luggage?	May ekstrang bayad hô ba ang bagahe?

Instructions

Continue!	Tulóy-tulóy lang hô.
The next street to the left/ right.	Pakaliwâ/Pakanan hô sa súsunód na kalye.
Please slow down.	Pakibagalan nga hô niyó.
Please wait here.	Pakihintáy hô dito.
Stop here!	Para na hô dito!
Stop at the corner.	Para na hô sa kanto.

BOAT

Where does the boat leave from?	Mulá hô saán áalís ang barkó?
What time does the boat arrive?	Anóng oras hô dáratíng ang barkó?
Is it safe to get off the boat while it's dark?	Delikado hô bang bumabá ng barkó habang madilím pa?

Useful Phrases

How long does the trip take?	Gaanó hô katagál ang biyahe?
Is it a direct route?	Diretsong ruta hô ba yón?
Is that seat taken?	May nakaupô na hô ba diyán?
I want to get off at ...	Bábabâ hô ako sa ...

CAR

International traffic signs are used in the Phillipines.

Where can I rent a car?	Saán hô maáring umupa ng awto?
How much is it daily/weekly?	Magkano hô kung arawán/lingguhan?
Does that include insurance/mileage?	Kasama na hô ba doón ang insiyurans/kilumetrahe?
Where's the next petrol station?	Saán hô ang pinakamalapit na gásolinahan?
Please fill the tank.	Pakipunô nga hô ang tanké.
I'd like ... litres.	... litro nga hô.
Please check the ...	Pakitignán lang hô ang ...
oil	langís
water	tubig
tyre pressure	ang hangin sa gulóng
Can I park here?	Puwéde ho báng pumarada dito?
How long can we park here?	Gaano katagál hô kami puwedeng pumarada dito?
Does this road lead to ...?	Patungo hô ba itóng daán na itó sa ...?

air	hangin
battery	bateryá
brakes	preno
clutch	klats
driver's licence	lisénsiya
engine (car)	mákina
garage	talyér
indicator	indikéytor; ilaw pang-senyas
leaded/regular	super/regulár

lights	mgá ilaw
main road	pangunahing kalye
oil	langís
puncture	butas
radiator	radyetor
roadmap	mapa ng daán
seatbelt	seatbelt; sinturóng pangseguro
self-service	self-service
speed limit	takdáng tulin
tyres	mgá gulóng
unleaded	regular
windscreen	windshield; panangga ng hangin

Car Problems

We need a mechanic.	Kailángan hô namin ng mekánikó.
What make is it?	Ano hô ang marká nitó?
The car broke down at ...	Nasiráan hô kamí ng awto sa ...
The battery is flat.	Patáy hô ang bateryá.
The radiator is leaking.	Tumutulò hô ang radyetor.
I have a flat tyre.	Na-platán hô akó ng gulóng.
It's overheating.	Nag-iinit hô.
It's not working.	Hindi hô gumagana.
I've lost my car keys.	Nawalá hô ang susì ng kotse ko.
I've run out of petrol.	Náubusan hô akó ng gasolina.

BICYCLE

Is it within cycling distance?	Maráratíng hô ba ng bisikleta?
Where can I hire a bicycle?	Saán hô puwedeng umarkilá ng bisikleta.
Where can I find secondhand bikes for sale?	Saán hô ba nakákabilí ng segunda manong bisikleta?
I've got a flat tyre.	Na-platán hô akó ng gulóng.

How much is it for ...?	Magkano hô ang upa para sa isáng ...
an hour	oras
the morning/afternoon	umaga/hapon
the day	araw

bike	bisikleta
brakes	preno
to cycle	magbisikleta
gear stick	kámbiyó
handlebars	manibela ng bisikleta
helmet	helmet
inner tube	interyór
lights	mgá ilaw
mountain bike	mountain bike
padlock	kandado
pump	bomba
puncture	butas
racing bike	reyser
saddle	úpuan
tandem	bisiklétang pangdalawahan
wheel	gulóng

ACCOMMODATION

It is very easy to find accommodation anywhere in the country. There is a wide range of hotels, motels, inns and townhouses in metropolitan Manila. In the remote areas in the provinces, it might be possible to arrange to live with families for a small fee and your friendship, if you are willing to rough it with them.

FINDING ACCOMMODATION

I'm looking for a ...	Nagháhanáp hô akó ng ...
camping ground	kampingan
guesthouse	bahay para sa mgá turista
hotel	otél
motel	motél
youth hostel	youth hostel
Where can I find a ...?	Saán hô may ...?
good hotel	mabuting otél
nearby hotel	otél na malapit dito
clean hotel	malinis na otél
Where's the ... hotel?	Saán hô ang ... otél dito?
best	pinakamabuting
cheapest	pinakamurang
What's the address?	Ano hô ang adrés?
Could you write the address, please?	Pakísulat niyó ngâ ang adrés.

ACCOMMODATION

BOOKING AHEAD

I'd like to book a room, please.	Gústo ko hong magreserba ng kuwarto.
Do you have any rooms available?	May bakante hô ba kayó?
For (three) nights.	Para sa (tatlóng) gabí hô.
How much for ...?	Magkano hô para sa ...?
one night	isáng gabí
a week	isáng linggó
two people	dalawáng táo
We'll be arriving at ...	Dáratíng hô kamí sa ...
My name is ...	... hô ang pangalan ko.
Does it include breakfast?	Kasama na hô ba doón ang almusál?

CHECKING IN

Do you have any rooms available?	May bakante hô ba kayó?
Sorry, we're full.	Sori hô, punô na kamí.
Do you have a room with two beds?	May kuwarto hô ba kayó na may dalawáng kama?
Do you have a room with a double bed?	May kuwarto hô ba kayó na may kamang pangdalawahan?
I'd like ...	Gústo ko hô ...
to share a dorm	na makisunong sa isáng malakíng kuwarto
a single room	ng páng-isahan na kuwarto
Can I see it?	Máaarì ko hô bang tignán?
Are there any others?	Meron pa hô bang ibá?
Where's the bathroom?	Násaán hô ba ang banyo?

We want a room with a ...	Gústo hô namin ng kuwarto na may ...
bathroom	banyo
shower	dutsa
TV	TV
window	bintanà

How much for ...?	Magkano hô para sa ...
one night	isáng gabí
a week	isáng linggó
two people	dalawáng tao

Is there hot water all day?	May mainit na tubig hô ba sa buóng araw?
Is there a discount for children/students?	May tawad hô ba para sa batà/istudyante?
It's fine. I'll take it.	Sige hô. Kukunin ko.

Requests & Complaints

I need a (another) ...	Kailangan ko hô ng (ng isá pang) ...
Do you have a safe where I can leave my valuables?	May kaha de yero hô ba kayó na mapaglalagyan ko ng aking mahahalagáng bagay?
Could I have a receipt for them?	Puwede hô ba akóng humingî ng resibo para sa mgá iyán.
Is there somewhere to wash clothes?	Saán hô puwedeng maglabá ng damít?
Can we use the telephone?	Máaari hô ba naming gamitin ang teléponó?
Please put some drinking water in my room.	Pakidalá nga hô ng tubig na ínumin sa aking kuwarto.
My room is too dark.	Masyadong madilím hô itóng aking kuwarto.

ACCOMMODATION

It's too cold/hot.	Masyadong magináw/mainit hô.
It's too noisy.	Masyadong maingay hô.
I can't open/close the window.	Hindî ko hô mabuksán/ masarhán ang bintanà.

This ... isn't clean.	Hindi hô yatà malinis itóng ...
blanket/sheet	blangket/kumot
pillow/pillow case	unan/punda

Please change it.	Pakipalitán nga hô itó.
Please change them.	Pakipalitán nga hô ang mgá itó.

CHECKING OUT

Can I pay with a travellers' cheque?	Puwede hô bang magbayad ng travellers' cheque?
Could I have the bill please?	Pakibigáy niyó ngâ sa akin ang kuwenta?
There's a mistake in the bill.	May malí hô yatà sa kuwenta.

Useful Words

air-conditioning	erkon
clean	malinis
key	susì
(bar of) soap	(bareta ng) sabón
face cloth	bimpo
lamp	lamsyed
lock	kandado
mosquito coil	katól
toilet	kubeta/CR/ toilet
toilet paper	tisyu
towel	tuwalya
water (cold/hot)	(malamíg/mainit na) túbig

> ### ng!
> The 'ng' sound as in 'ring' can also be at the beginning of Pilipino words.
> 'Ng' is also a separate letter and has its own entry in the dictionary which comes after the letter 'n'

PAPERWORK

Forms are normally in English and Pilipino but here are the translations of the entries anyway.

name	pangalan
address	tírahan
date of birth	petsa ng pagsilang
place of birth	lugár na sinilangan
age	edád/gulang
sex	kasarián
nationality	nasyonalidád
religion	relihiyón
profession/work	propesyón/trabaho
reason for travel	dahilán ng páglakbay
marital status	may asawa o walâ
single	binatà (m)/dalaga (f)
married	may asawa/kasál
divorced	hiwaláy
widow/widower	balo
identification	ID (English letters)
passport number	bilang ng pasport
visa	bisa
baptismal certificate	partída de bautismo
driving licence	lisensiya sa pagmamaneho
customs	adwana
immigration	imigrasyón
purpose of visit	dahilán ng paglakbay
holiday	para magbakasyón
business	para mangalakal
visiting relatives	para magbisita ng kamág-anak
visiting the homeland	para magbalíkbayan

CROSSWORD – ACCOMMODATION

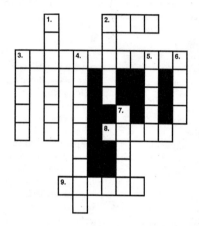

Across

2. Official approval for visiting a country
3. The price you hope you're being charged
8. Getting a wash standing up
9. Try finding this one-handed in the bath (first word)

Down

1. Typically rectangular space in a wall
2. Wash the front of your head with this
3. Protection for pillows
4. Place to pitch a tent
5. 10 Downing St, Beverley Hills 90210 (for example)
6. '*Let's Spend the ... Together*' - Rolling Stones
7. Pieces of cloth for sleeping on

AROUND TOWN

LOOKING FOR ...

Where is a ...?	Saán hô may ...?
bank	bangko
cinema	sinehán
consulate	konsulado
embassy	embahada
library	aklatan
market	palengke
museum	museo
police station	istasyón ng pulís
post office	pos opis
public telephone	teléponó
public toilet	comfort room/CR/ pálikuran
town square	plasa

AT THE BANK

You'll find that English terms are used in banks.

Can I use my credit card to withdraw money?	Puwede ko hô bang gamitin ang credit card ko para kumuha ng pera?
Can I exchange money here?	Máaarì hô bang magpalít ng pera dito?
Please write it down.	Pakisulat nga hô.
Can I have smaller notes?	Puwede niyó ba akóng bigyán ng mas maliliít kaysa diyán?
The automatic teller swallowed my card.	Kinain hô ng automatic teller ang aking kard.

I want to change ...	Gústo ko hong magpapalít ng ...
cash/money	pera
a cheque	tseke
a travellers' cheque	travellers check

What time does the bank open?
Anóng oras hô nagbúbukás ang bangko?

Where can I cash a travellers' cheque?
Saán hô akó maaring magpakás ng travellers check?

What's the exchange rate?
Magkano hô ang halagá ng pálitan?

Can I transfer money here from my bank?
Puwede hô ba akóng maglipat ng pera dito mulâ sa aking bangko?

How long will it take to arrive?
Gaanó hô katagál ba bago dumatíng iyón?

Has my money come yet?
Dumatíng na hô ba ang pera ko?

banknote	perang papél
change	suklî
coins	sinsilyo
small change	baryá

DID YOU KNOW ... Although you might find it distasteful, cockfights (sabong) are a popular attraction on most Sundays and public holidays. Something to watch for if you attend a sabong is the sign language that the book-keepers (kristos) use for betting. Nothing is written down as they commit all to memory.

AT THE POST OFFICE

If you're not sure how to ask for something, use the English term and it is likely that you will be understood.

I want to buy ...
   postcards
   stamps

Pagbilhán ninyó ngâ akó ng ...
   poskard
   sélyo

I want to send a ...
   aerogram
   letter
   parcel
   telegram

Gústo ko hóng magpadalá ng ...
   aerogram
   sulat
   pakete
   telegrama

Please send it by ...
How much does it cost
   to send this to ...?

Pakipadalá nga hô itó ng ...
Magkano hô kung ipápadalá
   ko itó sa ...?

air mail	ermeyl
envelope	sobre
express mail	ekspres
mail box	busón/hulugán ng sulat
parcel	pakete
pen	bolpen
postcode	post code
registered mail	registered
surface mail	surface mail

TELECOMMUNICATIONS

Could I please use the telephone?	Puwede ko hô bang gamitin ang teléponó?
I want to call ...	Gústo ko hóng tawagan ...
The number is ...	... hô ang número.
How much does a three-minute call cost?	Magkano hô ang tawag na tatlóng minuto?
I want to make a long-distance call to (Australia).	Gústo ko hong tumawag ng long-distance sa (Australya).
I want to make a reverse-charges/collect call.	Gústo ko hóng tumáwag na ang magbabayad ay ang kabilá.
What's the area code for ...?	Anó hô ba ang area code ng ...?
It's engaged.	Okupado hô ang linya.
I've been cut off.	Naputulan ho akó ng linya.
Is there a local Internet café?	Meron ho bang lokál na Internet Cafe dito?
I need to get Internet access.	Kailangan ko hong ma-access ang Internet.
Where can I use email?	Saán hô kayâ akó makakagamit ng email?
I need to check my email.	Kailangan ko hóng tignán ang email ko.
I want to send a fax.	Gústo ko hóng magpadalá ng fax.

operator	teleponista
phone book	librong pang-teléponó
phone box	public telephone
phonecard	kard pang-teléponó
telephone	teléponó
urgent	ápurahan

ON THE STREETS

What's this/that?	Anó hô itó/iyán?
What's happening (there)?	Anó hô ang nangyayari (doón)?
What happened (here)?	Anó hô ang nangyari (dito)?
What's s/he doing?	Anó hô ang ginágawâ niyá?
What's s/he selling?	Anó hô ang tinitindá niyá?
How much does this/ that cost?	Magkano hô itó/iyán?
How much do you charge?	Magkanong kubrá niyó?
Can I have one, please.	Bigyán niyó ngâ akô ng isá.
Is this for sale?	Pinagbíbilí hô ba itó?
Can I buy it?	Puwede ko hô bang bilhín itó?
Will you sell it to me?	Pagtítindá niyó ba itó sa akin?

sidewalk vendor	saydwok bendor
cigarette vendor	sigaret bendor
ambulant peddler	maglalakô
street urchin	watch your car boy
beggar	pulubi
policeman	pulís

AROUND TOWN

As it is in many cities all over the world, there are many pick-pockets, con artists and shysters in the streets of Manila. It might be a good idea to go around with someone who knows the city. Always keep your things close to you, or they might get lost.

Note: If approached by a beggar (old) and you are unable to give alms, you say: **Patatawarin po**, which is something like a very polite 'pardon me' or 'please forgive me'.

If you're merely looking and have no intentions of buying, then do just that , don't handle the wares. The vendors in the streets can be very persistent if they think you're interested. To get away from such street vendors, it's best to say with a smile; **Hindi hô. Saká na láng** ('No, maybe later'), and just walk away.

SIGNS

MAÍNIT/MAGINAW	HOT/COLD
PASUKÁN	ENTRANCE
LÁBASAN	EXIT
BAWAL PUMASOK	NO ENTRY
BAWAL MANIGARÍLYO	NO SMOKING
BUKÁS/SARADO	OPEN/CLOSED
BAWAL	PROHIBITED
CR	TOILETS
BAWAL BUMÚSINA	NO TOOTING OF HORN

Making a Call

Hello, is ... there?
Helo, nandiyán hô ba si ...

Hello. (answering a call)
Helo.

May I speak to ...?
Máaarì hô bang makausap si ...?

Who's calling?
Sino hô ba itó?

It's ...
Si ... hô. (pol)/Si ... (inf)

Yes, he/she is here.
Ohô/Oo, nandito siyá. (pol/inf)

One moment, (please).
Sandalî lang hô.

I'm sorry, he's not here.
Sori, walá hô siyá dito. (pol)
Sori, walâ siyá dito. (inf)

What time will she be back?
Anóng oras hô kayâ siyá babalík?

Can I leave a message?
Puwede hô bang magbilin?

Please tell her I called.
Pakísabi nga hô sa kanyá na
tumawag akó.

I'll call back later.
Tatawag hô ulî akó mamayâ.

SIGHTSEEING

Where's the tourist office?
Násaán hô ba ang tanggapan
ng turismo?

Do you have a local map?
May mapa hô ba kayó ng
lugár na itó?

AROUND TOWN

I'd like to see ...	Gústo ko hông makita ang ...
What time does it open/close?	Anóng oras hô itó nagbúbukás/nagsásará?
What's that building?	Ano hô ba ang gusalì na iyón?
What's this monument?	Anó hô ba ang monumentong itó?
May we take photographs?	Puwede hô ba kamíng kumuha ng litrato?
I'll send you the photograph.	Pápadalán ko hô kayó nitóng litrato.
Could you take a photograph of me?	Puwede ninyó/mo akóng kunan ng litrato? (pol/inf)

bridge	tuláy
church/cathedral	simbahan/katedrál
cinema	sinehán
concert	konsiyerto
crowded	masikíp
library	aklatan
monumento	monumento
mosque	moske
museum	museo
palace	palasyo
park	parke
statue	istatwa
university	unibersidád/pámantasan

AROUND TOWN

CROSSWORD – AROUND TOWN

Across

2. Tobacco pusher (first word)
4. Traditional hub of retail commerce
6. Trader on foot
8. Forbidden by law
9. Cross between official building and private home

Down

1. Place where books and other literature is kept
2. Currency that jangles
3. Easiest way of crossing a river
5. Institution representing a foreign country
7. Traditional civic centre

GOING OUT

WHERE TO GO

What's there to do in the evenings?	Anó ho ba ang puwedeng gawin dito sa gabí para maglibáng?
I'd like to go to ... a bar/café a cinema a jazz/karaoke bar a night club the theatre a concert a disco a restaurant that serves native dishes	Gústo ko hóng pumuntá sa ... bar/café sinehán jazz/karaoke bar nayt klab teatro konsiyerto disko restaurán na naghahandà ng mga katutubong pagkain
I'd like to watch a ... local pop group	Gústo ko hóng manoód ng ... pagtatanghál ng isang local pop group
performance of folk dances Pilipino film	pagtatanghál ng mgá katutubong sayáw pelíkuláng Pilipino
Is there a cover charge?	May bayad hô ba ang pagpasok?
How much is the cover charge?	Magkano hô ang bayad pagpasok?
Where can I find out what's on?	Saán ko malaman kung saán may happening?
Is there an entertainment guide?	Meron bang entertainment guide?

I'd like two tickets for ...
please.
   the show
   this evening
   tomorrow night

Pakibigyán niyó ngâ ako ng
dalawang tiket para sa ...
   sa palabás
   ngayóng gabí
   bukas

ARRANGING TO MEET

When should we meet?	Kelan ba tayo magkikita?
Where should we meet?	Saán tayo magkikita?
Would ... o'clock be fine?	Ayos ba ang alas ...?
That's fine.	Ayos.
Shall we have dinner together?	Puwede ba tayong mag-dinner?
Shall we go dancing?	Puwede ba tayong mag-disco?
See you later.	Sige.
See you on (Friday).	Magkita tayo sa (Biyernes).
Sorry I'm late.	Sori, hulí akó.

CLASSIC PICK-UP LINES

Haven't we met before?	Nakilala na kitá, di ba?
Would you like a cigarette?	Gústo mo ng sigarilyo?
Would you like to dance?	Gústo mo bang magsayaw?
I like you very much.	Gustóng-gústo kitá.
Do you like me too?	Gústo mo rin ba akó?
You look great!	Ang ganda mo!
May I kiss you?	Puwede ba kitáng halikán?
Can I call you?	Puwede ba kitáng tawagan?

GOING OUT

CLASSIC REJECTIONS

Get Lost!	Alís diyán!
Do you mind!	Puwede ba!
I'm not on my own.	May kasama akó.
You're not my type.	Hindî kitá tipo.
I don't want to get involved.	Ayokong ma-involve.
I'm gay.	Gay ako.
No, thank you.	Hindî salamat na lang.
I'm waiting for someone.	May hinihntay akó.
I'm happy on my own thanks.	Salamat na lang, mas gústo kong nagíisá.
I'm not interested.	Hindi akó interesado.
Leave me alone!	Puwede ba, pabayaan mo akó!

DATING & ROMANCE
Breaking the Ice

Do you mind if I sit here?	Máaring tumabí.
Can I buy you a drink?	Puwede ba kitáng ikuha ng máinóm?
Do you want to dance?	Gústo mo bang magsayaw?
Do you have a boyfriend/ girlfriend?	Merong ka bang nobyo/ nobya?
Here's my telephone number.	Étong número ng teléponó ko.
I'd like to see you again.	Gústo kitang makita ulí.

Useful Words & Phrases

Let's go dutch.	Kani-kanyang bayad.
Who's shouting?	Sinong tayâ?
My treat/My shout.	Akóng tayâ.

GOING OUT

I'm not drunk.	Hindî akó lasíng. (pol)
I'm not yet drunk.	Hindî pa akó lasíng. (inf)
The night is still young.	Maaga pang gabí.
Let's go bar-hopping.	Magbar-hopping tayo.
Don't be a spoilsport.	Huwág kang KJ.
It's late.	Gabing-gabi na.
drunk	lasing

Afterwards

It was nice talking to you.	Enjoy akóng magkipagusap sa iyó.
It was nice to meet you.	Masaya akóng nakilala ka.
I have to go now.	Kailangan na akóng umalís.
I had a great day/night.	Nag-enjóy akó ngayóng araw/gabi.
I hope to see you again soon.	Sana Magkita ulí tayo.
I'll give a you call.	Tatawag akó.
See you soon.	Hanggang sa mulî.
We must do this again.	Sa úulitin.

COMMON INTERESTS

What do you do in your spare time?	Papano ka nagpapalipas ng panahón kapág walá kang ginagawa? (inf)
I like ...	Gústo kong ...
I don't like ...	Ayaw kong ...
Do you like ...?	Mahilig ba kayó sa ...? (pol)
	Mahilig ka ba sa ...? (inf)

film	pelíkulá
music	músika
sport	ispórt
art	sining
the theatre	teatro
photography	potograpiya
food	pagkain

Do you like ...?	Mahilig ba kayóng ...? (pol)
	Mahilig ka báng ...? (inf)

going out	magpasyál
playing games	maglarô
playing soccer	maglarô ng soccer
playing sport	maglarô ng ispórt
reading books	magbasá ng libró
shopping	mamilí
travelling	magbiyahe
watching TV	manoód ng TV
dancing	magsayáw
going to the disco	mag-disko
cooking	maglutò
writing	magsulát

INTERESTS

The phrases below are in the informal forms only.

What do you enjoy doing?	Anóng hilig mong gawín?
I enjoy ...	Mahilig akóng ...
I don't enjoy ...	Hindî akó mahilig ...
just staying home	na nasa bahay lang
going out	mamasyál
inviting friends over	magimbitá ng mga kaibigan
listening to music	makiníg sa músika
working in the garden	maghardín
tending to my pet animals	mag-alagà ng mgá alagà kong hayop
studying	mag-aral
studying languages	mag-aral ng mgá wika
shopping	mamilí
playing sport	maglaró ng ispórt
fixing things	mag-kumponé ng mgá bagay
collecting things	mangulekta ng mgá bagay

FAMILY

Filipinos are very family-oriented and you'll find that they enjoy talking about their family immensely. A Filipino family can be made up of the father, the mother, the children, grandparents, aunts and uncles, nephews and nieces and so on. So be prepared for a long conversation if you engage Filipinos in a conversation about their family.

Are you married?	May asawa na ba kayó? (pol)
	May asawa ka na ba? (inf)
I'm single.	Walâ pa hô akong asáwa. (pol)
	Walâ pa akóng asawa. (inf)
I'm married.	May asawa na hô akó. (pol)
	May asawa na akó. (inf)

INTERESTS

How many children do you have?	Ilán ang anák niyó? (pol) Ilán ang anák mo? (inf)
We don't have any children.	Walâ pa hô kamíng anák. (pol) Walâ pa kamíng anák. (inf)
I have a ...	Meron hô akong ... (pol) Meron akóng ... (inf)
How many siblings do you have?	Ilán kayóng magkakapatíd?
Is your spouse here?	Nanditó ba ang asawa niyó/ mo? (pol/inf)
Do you have a boyfriend/ girlfriend?	May nobyo/nobya na ba kayó? (pol) May nobyo/nobya ka na ba? (inf)

sibling	kapatíd
brother	kapatíd na lalake
sister	kapatíd na babae
children	mgá anák
family	pamilya/mag-anak
husband	asawa/táo
wife	asawa/maybahay
parents	mgá magulang
father	tatay
mother	nanay
older brother	kuya
older sister	ate

I LIKE IT

The word gústo is
used to express
'I like ...' or 'I want ...'

It must be noted,
however, that gústo is
not a verb.

INTERESTS

son/daughter	anák na lalake/babae
uncle	tiyo
aunt	tiya
nephews and nieces	mgá pamangkín
nephew	pamangkín na lalake
niece	pamangkín na babae
cousin	pinsan
grandfather	lolo
grandmother	lola
parents-in-law	mgá biyanán
father-in-law	biyenáng lalake
mother-in-law	biyenáng babae
brother-in-law	bayáw
sister-in-law	hipag

MAKING CONVERSATION

The phrases below are in the informal form.

Where can you take a walk here?	Saán puwedeng mamasyál dito?
What do you do when you just stay home?	Anú-anó naman ang ginágawâ mo kapág nasa bahay ka lang?
What do you plant in your garden?	Anó namán ang tinátaním mo sa iyóng hardin?
flowering plants	mgá halamang namúmulaklák
vegetables	mgá gulay

I ...	Akóy ...
cook	naglulutò
listen to the radio	nakikiníg sa radyo
watch TV	nanónoód ng TV
read (books, magazines, comics)	nagbábasá (ng libró, mgá mágasín, mgá komiks)
write letters	sumusulat ng mgá liham

Do you have ...	Meron ka bang ...
a pet dog	alagang aso
a pet cat	alagang pusà
a pet bird	alagang ibon
a pet horse	alagang kabayo
goats	mgá kambíng
pigs	mgá baboy

Do you like sport?	Mahilíg ka ba sa ispórt?
I like playing sport.	Mahilig akóng maglaró ng ispórt.

Do you play ...?	Naglalarô ka ba ng ...?
tennis	tenis
basketball	basketbol
football	putbol
table tennis	pingpong
baseball	beysbol
softball	sopbol
golf	golp

I prefer to watch rather than play sport.	Mas gústo kong manoód lang kaysa sumali.
That sport is popular/not popular in my country.	Populár/Hindî populár ang ispórt na yán sa aking bayan.

INTERESTS

INTERESTS

That sport is not known in our country.	Hindî kilalá ang ispórt na yán sa aming bayan.
What languages are you interested in?	Sa anú-anóng wikà ka interesado?
I like talking to people.	Mahílig akong makipág-usap sa mga táo.
Do you collect stamps?	Nangungulekta ka ba ng mgá selyo?

Useful Phrases

It's a/an ... hobby.	... na libangan iyán.
expensive	magastos
enjoyable	nakákatuwâ
time-consuming	magastos sa panahón
boring	nakákayamót
I have no time to indulge in hobbies.	Walâ akong panahón para sa libangan.
It's a good hobby for ...	Magalíng na libangan iyan para sa ...
young people	kabataan
old people	mgá matatandâ
men	mgá lalake
women	mgá babae

SHOPPING

LOOKING FOR ...

You can get almost anything you need in the shops in Manila as there are huge shopping malls everywhere.

The phrases given below are in the informal form.

Where can I buy ...?	Saán ako makákabilí ng ...?
Where's the nearest ...?	Násaán ang pinakamalapit na ...?
general store	tindahan
barber	barberiya
bookshop	tindahan ng libró
chemist/pharmacy	botika/parmasya
clothing store	tindahan ng damit
laundrette	laundromat
market	palengke
souvenir shop	tindahan ng subenir
neighbourhood variety store	sari-sari istor
bakery	panaderyá
shoe shop	tindahan ng sapatos
tailor	sastré
dressmaker	modista

MAKING A PURCHASE

I'd like to buy ...	Gústo ko hóng bumili ng ...
Do you have others?	Meron hô pa ba kayóng iba?
I don't like it.	Ayoko nitó.
Can I look at it?	Puwede bang tignán?
I'm just looking.	Tumítingín lang hô akó.

How much is this?	Magkano hô itó?
Can you write down the price?	Pakisulat ngâ niyó ang presyo.
Do you accept credit cards?	Tumátanggáp ba kayó ng credit card?
Please wrap it.	Pakibalot nga hô.

BARGAINING

It's fine to bargain in the smaller shops and in the markets. The tip is to size up the vendor and the merchandise, before starting to haggle. If you shop early, you'll find that the vendors will give in easily to your haggling because of a Filipino belief that an early pleasant sale will ensure good sales throughout the rest of the day. This belief is called **buena mano**, literally meaning 'good hand' in Spanish.

I think it's too expensive!	Ang mahál-mahál namán!
It's too much for us.	Hindî hô namin kaya iyán.
Can you lower the price?	May tawad hô ba iyán?
	Puwede hong tumawad?
Is there something cheaper than that?	May mas murá-murá hô ba kaysa riyán?
Give it to me at my price.	Ibigáy na niyó sa tawad ko.

PRICES

The Philippine currency is the peso and centavo, from the Spanish. In Pilipino, however, it is the piso and sentimo. Prices over 10 are usually given in Spanish numbers but they are often also given in English.

three pesos	tatlóng piso
five centavos	limáng séntimó
15 pesos	kínse pésos
40 pesos	kuwarenta pesos
four pesos and 50 centavos	four fifty

For quantities, Pilipino numbers are used. Spanish numbers may also be used.

How much for ...?	Magkano ang ...?
a hundred	isandaán
a dozen	isang dosena
half a dozen	kalahating dosena
five litres (eg. petrol)	singko litros/limáng litro

ESSENTIAL GROCERIES

Where can I find ...?	Saán merong ...?
I'd like to buy ...	Gústo kong bumilí ng ...
bread	tinapay
butter	mantekilya
cheese	keso
chocolate	tsokolate
eggs	itlóg
flour	arina
gas cyclinder	tanké ng gas
ham	hamón
honey	pulút-pukyutan

SHOPPING

margarine	margarina
matches	pósporó
milk	gatas
pepper	pamintá
salt	asín
shampoo	syampu
soap	sabón
sugar	asukal
toilet paper	tisyu/papél sa kubeta
toothpaste	tutpeyst
washing powder	sabong panlaba
yoghurt	yoghurt

SHOPPING

THEY MAY SAY ...

Ano hô ba ang kailangan niyó?	Can I help you?
Iyán na lang hô ba?	Will that be all?
Murang-mura na hô iyán.	That's very cheap.
Sori, nag-íisá na lang hô ito.	Sorry, this is the only one I have.
Ilán hô ba ang gústo niyó?	How many would you like?
Anó hô ang sukat niyó?	What size are you?
Kasya ho ba?	Does it fit?
Bagay na bagay hô.	It's very becoming.
Walá hong tawad diyán.	I can't give you a discount on that.
Kúkunin ba niyó?	Are you going to take it?

SOUVENIRS

baskets	mgá basket
brassware	kasangkapang yaring-tansò
cane ware/furniture	sulihiyá/muwebles na gawâ sa uwáy
handicraft	mgá bagay na yaring- kamáy
woodcarved figure	statuwáng inukit
souvenirs made of shell	subenir na gawâ sa kabibi
jewellery	alahas
ring	singsíng
bracelet	pulseras
necklace	kuwintás
earrings	hikaw
leathergoods	mgá bagay na yarì sa balát
poster	paskíl

CLOTHING

jacket	diyaket
jumper (sweater)	pulober (suweter)
pants	pantalón
raincoat	kapote
shirt	kamisadentro
shoes	sapatos
socks	medyas
swimsuit	damít panligò
T-shirt	kamiseta
underwear	damit panloób
singlet	sando
boxer shorts	karsonsilyo
panty	salawál
slippers	tsinelas
dress	barò
skirt	palda
blouse	blusa
jeans	maóng

SHOPPING

MATERIALS

cloth	tela
cotton	koton
silk	seda
linen	de-ilo
unbleached muslin cloth	katsâ
embroidered	burdado
crocheted	ginanatsilyo
knitted	niniting
ceramic	serámikó
handmade	yarì sa kamáy/gawá sa kamáy
glass	kristá
leather	balát
metal	metál
copper	tansô
of gold	na gintô
of silver	na pilak
wood	kahoy

COLOURS

colour	kulay
dark ...	matingkad na ...
light ...	murà na ...
black	itím
blue	asúl/bugháw
brown	kulay-kapé
green	berde
grey	kulay-abó
orange	kulay-dalandán
pink	rosas
purple	kulay-ube/lila

PLURAL

Nouns in Pilipino have the same form whether they are singular or plural.
However, you can tell if a noun is plural if it has the plural particle mgá before it, or simply by the context.

red	**pulá**
white	**putî**
yellow	**diláw**

TOILETRIES

condoms	**kondom**
deodorant	**pang-alís ng amóy**
moisturising cream	**moisturizing cream**
razor	**pang-ahit**
sanitary napkins	**tampon**
shampoo	**syampu**
shaving cream	**cream na pang-ahit**
soap	**sabón**
sunblock	**sunblock**
tampons	**tampon**
toilet paper	**tisyu/papél sa kubeta**

SHOPPING

DID YOU KNOW ... Remember that you should take at least a taste or so of food if someone offers it to you. However, you should always leave a little food on the plate to show that you've had plenty and that you're not greedy.

SHOPPING

FOR THE BABY

tinned baby food	pagkain ng batà na de lata
baby powder	gatas na pulbós na pambatà
bib	babero
disposable nappies	lampin ng batà na maáring itapon
dummy/pacifier	tsupón
feeding bottle	botelya ng batá
nappy	lampín
powdered milk	gatas na pulbós

STATIONERY & PUBLICATIONS

Is there an English-language bookshop here?	Meron hô bang tindahan ng libró sa wikang Inglés dito?
Is there an English-language section?	Meron hô bang lugár para sa wikang Inglés?
Is there a local entertainment guide?	Meron hô bang local entertainment guide?
newspaper in English	peryódikó sa wikang Inglés
paper	papél
pen (ballpoint)	bolpen
stamp	selyo

Do you sell ...?	Nagtitinda ba kayó ng ...?
magazines	mágasín
newspapers	peryódikó
foreign newspapers	banyagang peryódikó
postcards	poskard
dictionary	diksyunaryo
envelope	sobre

... map	mapa ...
city	ng siyudád
regional	pángrehiyón
road	ng kalye

MUSIC

The following phrases are in the informal form.

I'm looking for a ... CD.	Naghahanap akó ng ... C.D.
Do you have any ...?	Meron ba kayóng ...?
What's his/her best recording?	Anó ba ang pinakamagalíng na recording niyá?
I heard a band/singer called ...	May náriníg akóng banda/mang-ááwit na ang pangalan ay ...
Who's the best ballad singer?	Sino ang pinakamagalíng na mang-ááwit ng ballad?
What is the most popular rock group here?	Anóng pinakatanyág na rock group dito?
Can I listen to this CD here?	Puwede ko bang pakinggán itóng CD na itó dito?
I need a blank tape.	Kaílangan ko ng blangkong tape.

PHOTOGRAPHY

People working in photo shops will know the English words for
the terms used in this field.

How much is it to process this film?	**Magkano mágpagawá ng litrato?**
When will it be ready?	**Kelan hô makúkuha?**
I'd like a film for this camera.	**Gústo ko ng pilm para díto sa kámera.**
Can I have my passport photo taken?	**Puwedeng kunan niyó akó ng litrato para sa pasport?**
battery	**baterýa**
B&W film	**pilm na waláng kulay/ pelíkuláng waláng kulay**
camera	**kámera**
colour film	**pilm na may kulay**
film	**pilm/pelíkulá**
flash/flash bulb	**plas/plas balb**
lens	**lente**

SMOKING

The phrases below are in the informal form.

A packet of cigarettes, please.	**Isáng pakete ngâ ng sigarilyo.**
Are these cigarettes strong or mild?	**Matapang ba itóng sigarilyo o suwabe?**
Do you have a light?	**May sindí ka ba?**
Please don't smoke.	**Huwág ka ngang manigarilyo.**
Do you mind if I smoke?	**Okey lang ba sa iyó kung manigarilyo akó?**
I'm trying to give up.	**Sinúsubúkan kong tumigil.**

SHOPPING

cigarettes	sigarilyo/yosì
cigarette papers	papél para sa sigarilyo
filtered	may filter
lighter	lighter
matches	pósporó
menthol	mentol
pipe	kwako
tobacco	tabako

SIZES & COMPARISONS

small	maliít
big	malakí
heavy	mabigát
light	magaán
more	mas marami
little (amount)	kauntî
too much/many	masyadong marami
many	marami
enough	sapát
also	din
a little bit	katitíng

CROSSWORD – SHOPPING

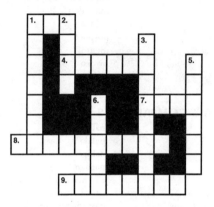

SHOPPING

Across

1. Impurities removed
4. Often used in combination with conditioner
7. Photoactive material in a camera
8. Churned cow juice
9. Chain ornament

Down

1. Couturier, as the French say
2. Cancer sticks
3. Oral hygiene agent
5. Hopefully you haven't worn these since babyhood
6. Ornament for dangly bits

FOOD

The Filipinos love their food and take advantage of every occasion to celebrate with a lavish amount of food in all its varieties. You'll be surprised to know how many meals Filipinos sit down to. They have breakfast in the morning, meryenda (snack) at mid-morning, lunch at noon, another meryenda in the afternoon and finally dinner in the evening.

| breakfast | almusál/agahan | dinner | hapunan |
| lunch | tanghalian | snack | meryenda |

VEGETARIAN & SPECIAL MEALS

The phrases below are in both polite and informal forms. If a sentence includes the particle hô and/or the polite pronouns kayó or ninyó (niyó) it is in the polite form.

I'm a vegetarian.	Gulay lamang ang kinakain ko.
I don't eat meat.	Hindî akó kumakain ng karné.
I don't eat chicken, fish or ham.	Hindî akó kumakain ng manók, isdâ o hamón.
I can't eat dairy products.	Hindî ako puwedeng kumain ng mgá pagkaing gawâ sa gatas.

I can't eat beef/pork.	Hindî akó puwedeng kumain ng karnéng-baka/ karnéng-baboy.
Do you have any vegetarian dishes?	Meron ba kayóng mgá ulam na gulay lang?
Does this dish have meat?	May karné ba itóng ulam na itó?
Can I get this without meat?	Puwede niyó kong bigyán nitóng ulam na itó na waláng karné?
Does it contain eggs?	May sahóg na itlóg ba itó?
I'm allergic to (peanuts).	May alerdyi akó sa (manî).
Is there a kosher restaurant here?	May restaurán bang kosher dito?
Is this kosher?	Kosher ba itó?
Is this organic?	Organic ba itó?

EATING OUT

Over the years numerous eating places of every kind have cropped up. It has become very much the thing to do for people to lunch or dine out on weekends with family or friends.

Table for (five), please.	Kailangan hô namin nang mesang (panlima).
May we see the menu?	Puwede hô bang makita ang menú?
Please bring some ...	Pakidalá ngâ ng ...
Do I get it myself or do they bring it to us?	Akó hô ba mismo ang kukuha o silá ang magdádalá dito sa amin?

FOOD

Please bring ...	Pakidalá nga hô ...
an ashtray	ng isáng sinisero
the bill	ang kuwenta/chit
a fork	ng isáng tinidór
a glass of water (with/without ice)	ng isáng basong tubig (na may yelo/na waláng yelo)
a knife	ng isáng kutsilyo
a plate	ng isáng plato

No ice in my beer, please. Huwág ninyóng lagyán ng yelo ang serbesa ko.

Is service included in the bill? Kasama ba ang serbisyo sa kuwenta?

Useful Words

bitter	mapaít
bowl	mangkók
cup	tasa
fork	tinidór
fresh	sariwà
glass	baso
jug	pitsél
knife	kutsilyo
plate	plato
platter	bandehado
salty	maálat
saucer	platito
serviette	sirbilyeta
sour	maásim
spicy	maangháng
spoon	kutsara
stale/spoiled	sirâ/panís
sweet	matamís
toothpick	tutpik

FOOD

TYPICAL DISHES

Adobo
One of the most popular Philippine dishes, it's made from chicken pieces or pork and cooked in a mixture of vinegar, garlic, salt, peppercorns, and sometimes bay leaves and soy sauce.

Atsára
A very healthy and vitamin rich side dish, the Philippine sauerkraut, made from pickled grated unripe papaya.

Calderéta
A dish of Spanish origin, it is a stew of goat's meat or beef, with peas and paprika.

Dinuguan
A dish made from finely chopped pork offal and diced pork stewed in fresh pig blood and vinegar and seasoned with hot peppers. It is usually served with **puto**, a white coloured native cake made from rice flour, and served as a **meryenda** ('snack').

Fish Kinilaw
Small pieces of fish marinated in vinegar, ginger and onions. In some regions in the Philippines, coconut milk is added to give it a rich flavour.

Inihaw na Lapu-Lapu
Grilled grouper, seasoned with salt, pepper, garlic and soy sauce. It's the most popular fish dish in the country, but is quite expensive.

FOOD

TYPICAL DISHES

Halo-Halò
A dessert made from shaved ice mixed with sweetened bananas, sweet potatoes, yam, black and white beans, agar-agar, fruits, smothered in evaporated milk and mixed together. Halo-halò literally means 'mix-mix', which is what you do to it before eating it.

Karé-Karé
A dish with ox tail, ox leg, string beans, eggplants and radish in broth, thickened by crushed roasted peanuts and rice. It has a sauce made from sauteed salted shrimp.

Lechon/Litson
Roasted suckling pig served with thick liver sauce. It's a popular fiesta dish.

Lumpiáng Sariwà
A spring roll filled with chopped coconut pith, chickpeas and shrimps. It's served with a slightly sweet sauce.

Pancit Cantón
A Chinese-influenced noodle dish which is a meal in itself. It has thick noodles, a variety of vegetables, pieces of chicken, pork and shrimps.

Sinigang na Hipon
A very light sour soup with prawns, kangkóng (spinach-like native leafy vegetable) leaves and tender stems. The stock is made sour by green tamarind.

Ukoy
An appetiser made from small shrimps fried in batter, served with a vinegar and garlic sauce.

FOOD

SELF-CATERING

When you are cooking for yourself and using western ingredients, especially in the cities, it's best to go to the supermarket. You will be surprised to find most, if not all, of the ingredients you need. If you want fresh food ingredients, go to the market. You can get these foods in the supermarket.

cooking oil	langís panluto
bread	tinapay
butter	mantikilya
cheese	keso
chocolate	tsokolate
coconut milk	gatâ
eggs	itlóg
fish sauce	patís
flour	arina
garlic	bawang
ginger	luya
ham	hamón
honey	pulút-pukyutan
lard	mantikà
margarine	margarina
(fresh) milk	(sariwang) gatas
condensed milk	kondensada
evaporated milk	ebaporada
onion	sibuyas
pepper	pamintá
salt	asín
soy sauce	toyò
sugar	asukal
tomatoes	kamatis
vinegar	sukà
yoghurt	yoghurt

FOOD

AT THE MARKET

It's best to go to the market early in the morning when everything is still fresh, the vendors are still nice and friendly and there aren't many people around.

MEAT & POULTRY

beef	karnéng-baka	meat	karné
chicken	manók	pork	karnéng-baboy
duck	pato	turkey	pabo
goatmeat	karnéng-kambing	venison	karnéng-usá

SEAFOOD

clams	tulyá
crabs, large and with thick dark shell	alimángo
crabs, smaller	talangkâ
crabs, spotted and thinner shelled	alimasag
lobster	uláng
mussels	tahóng
oysters	talabá
shrimp	hípon

FOOD

DID YOU KNOW ... Most spirits are often called wine in the Philippines so you might have trouble when you come to order wine. If you actually want red or white wine, you might have to try ordering 'grapes wine'.

VEGETABLES

bean sprouts	toge
beans	bataw
bitter melon	ampalayá
cassava	kamoteng kahoy
Chinese string beans	sitaw
eggplant	talóng
lima beans	patanì
mild radish-type vegetable	singkamás
ramie leaves	saluyot
spinach-like vegetable	kangkóng
squash	kalabasa
sweet potatoes	kamote
vegetables	gulay

FRUIT

avocado	abokádo
banana	saging
cantaloupe	milón
custard apple	atis
fruit	prutas
lime	dayap
mandarin	dalanghita
mango	manggá
orange	dalandan
papaya/pawpaw	papaya
pineapple	pinyá
pomelo	suhà
Spanish plum	sinigwélas
star apple	kaimíto
watermelon	pakwán

FOOD

guyabano
   fruit which looks like a jackfruit but with flesh and
   taste similar to custard apple

kalamansi
   small citrus fruit used for juice

lansones
   small yellow-skinned fruit in clusters with sweet
   lychee-like flesh

SPICES & CONDIMENTS

coconut milk	gatâ
garlic	bawang
ginger	luya
onions	sibuyas
peppers	sili
saffron	kasubhâ
salt	asín
small hot chilli peppers	labuyò

DRINKS

(cup of) tea	(isang tásang) tsaá
with/without milk	may/walang gatas
with/without sugar	may/walang asúkal
avocado drink	abokádo dyus
cocoa	tsokolate
coffee	kapé
ginger tea	salabát
lemonade	limonâda
mango drink	mango dyus

FOOD

water	tubig
boiled water	pinakuluáng tubig
cold water	malamíg na tubig
hot water	mainit na tubig
mineral water	mineral water

USEFUL WORDS & PHRASES

How much is (a kilo of) ...?	Magkano hô (ang isang kilo ng) ...?
rice	bigás
mangos	manggá
a slice of beef	ang isáng hiwà ng karné
a packet of soup	ang isáng pakete ng sopas
a carton of eggs	ang isáng kartón ng itlóg

Do you have anything cheaper?	Meron ba kayóng mas mura?
What's the local speciality?	Ano hô ang espesiyalidád sa lugár na itó?

What's this?	Anó hô itó?
May I taste it?	Puwede hong tikmán?

FOOD

IN THE COUNTRY

CAMPING

With more and more people getting into mountaineering, camping has become a popular holiday activity.

camping	pagkakampo/pagkakamping
campsite	kampuhan/kampingan
rope	lubid
tent	tolda
torch (flashlight)	lente
firewood	kahoy na panggatong
hammer	martilyo
hammock	duyan
mattress	kutsón
mat (native)	baníg
mosquite net	moskitero
stove	kalán
tent pegs	pako para sa tolda

Do you have any sites available?	Meron pa ba kayóng puwestong bakante?
How much is it per person/ per tent?	Magkano hô bawat táo/ tolda?
Where can I hire a tent?	Saán ho puwedeng umupa ng tolda?
Can we camp here?	Puwede ba kamíng magkamping dito?
Who owns this land?	Sino hô ang may-arì nitóng lupang itó?
Can I talk to him/her?	Puwede ko hô ba siyáng makausap?
Are there shower facilities?	Meron ho bang lugár na mapagliliguan?

HIKING & MOUNTAINEERING

Many young Filipinos are into mountaineering now and as you are more likely to talk with younger adults on the trail, the phrases below have been given in the informal form.

Are there any tourist attractions near here?	May mgá lugár na pangturista ba na malapit dito?
Where's the nearest village?	Násaán ang pinakamalapit na baryo?
Where can I find out about hiking trails in the region?	Saán akó makakaalám tungkol sa mgá daáng nilalakaran sa poók na itó?
Are there guided treks?	Meron bang mgá paglalakad na may giya?
I'd like to talk to someone who knows this area.	Gústo kong makipagusap sa sinumang kilalá itóng lugár na itó.
Do we need a guide?	Kailángan ba namin ng kasama/giya?
Is it safe to climb this mountain?	Hindî ba delikadong umakyát sa bundók na itó?
Is there a hut up there?	May kubo ba doón sa taás?
How long is the trail?	Gaano kahabà ang daán?
Is the track well marked?	Meron bang malilinaw na tandâ sa daán?
How high is the climb?	Gaano kataás ang pagakyát?
Which is the shortest route?	Alín ang pinakamaiklíng dáanan?

Which is the easiest route?	Alín ang pinakámadalíng dáanan?
Is the path open?	Bukás ba ang dáanan?
When does it get dark?	Kelan nagdídilím?
Is it very scenic?	Magandáng-magandá ba ang mga tanawin doón?
Where can I hire mountain gear?	Saán akó makaka-arkilá ng mgá kagamitáng pang-akyát sa bundók?
Where can we buy supplies?	Saán kamí makákabilí ng mgá kailangan namin?

On the Path

Where have you come from?	Saán ka nanggaling?
How long did it take you?	Gaano katagál ang lakad mulâ doón?
Does this path go to ...?	Papuntá ba itóng daán na itó sa ...?
I'm lost.	Nawawalâ akó.
Where can we spend the night?	Saán kamí máaaring magpalipas ng gabí?
Can I leave some things here for a while?	Puwedeng iwanan ko sandalí ang iláng bagay dito?
altitude	tayog
backpack	backpack

IN THE COUNTRY

binoculars	lárgabista
candles	mgá kandilà
to climb	umakyát/akyatín
compass	kumpas
downhill	palusóng/pababâ
first-aid kit	first-aid kit
gloves	mgá guwantes
guide	giya
guided trek	paglalakad na may giya
hiking	malayuang paglalakad
hiking boots	mgá botas na pang-lakad
hunting	pangangaso
ledge	ungóy
lookout	tanod/bantay
map	mapa
mountain climbing	pamumundók
pick	piko
provisions	mgá baon

rock climbing
  pagaakyát sa bató
rope
  lubid
signpost
  posteng panandâ
steep
  matarik
trek
  paglalakád
uphill
  paakyát
to walk
  maglakád'/lumakad

GLOTTAL STOPS

Vowels that are
marked with a ( ) or a
( ) are pronounced
with a glottal stop
following them.
For a more detailed
explanation on glottal
stops see page 17.

AT THE BEACH

Can we swim here?	Puwede ba kamíng lumangóy dito?
Is it safe to swim here?	Hindí ba delikadong lumangóy díto?
What time is high/low tide?	Anóng oras ang pagtaog/pagkati ditó?

coast	baybáy-dagat
fishing	pangingisdâ
reef	bahura/batuhán
rock	batuhán
sand	buhangin
sea	dagat
snorkelling	snorkelling
sunblock	pampahid sa balat na pangsanggá sa sinag ng araw
sunglasses	sanglas
surf	daluyong
surfing	surfing
surfboard	surfboard
swimming	paglangóy
towel	tuwalya
waterskiing	water-skiing
waves	alon
windsurfing	windsurfing

Diving

scuba diving	pagsisisid; scuba diving
Are there good diving sites here?	Meron bang mahuhusay na lugár dito na mapag-iiscuba diving?

IN THE COUNTRY

Can we hire a diving boat/ guide?	Puwede ba kaming umupa ng bangkâ na pangsisid/giya?
We'd like to hire diving equipment.	Gústo naming umarkilá ng mgá kasangkapang pangsisid.
I'm interested in exploring wrecks.	Interesado akóng magsiyasat ng labí ng mga bapór.

WEATHER

What's the weather like?	Anóng lagáy ng panahón?
Today it's ...	... ngayon.
cloudy	maulap
cold	magináw
hot	mainit
warm	medyo mainit
windy	mahangin
It's raining heavily.	Malakás ang ulán.
It's raining lightly.	Umáambón.
It's flooding.	Bumábahâ.
monsoon season	panahón ng bagyó
storm	bagyó/unos
sun	araw
typhoon	bagyó

GEOGRAPHICAL TERMS

beach	apláya
bridge	tuláy
cave	kwéba
cliff	talabís
earthquake	lindól
farm	bukid
footpath	dáanan
forest	gubat
gap/narrow pass	makítid na daán
harbour	dáungan
hill	buról/munting bundók
hot spring	bukal ng maínit na túbig
island	pulò
lake	lawà
mountain	bundók
mountain path	dáanan sa bundók
pass	landás
peak	tuktók/taluktók
river	ilog
sea	dagat
valley	lambák
waterfall	talón

Seasons

summer	tag-inít/tag-aráw
autumn	taglagás
winter	taglamig
spring	tagsibol
dry season	tag-aráw/tagtuyót
rainy season	tag-ulán
season	panahón

IN THE COUNTRY

FAUNA
Birds

bird	ibon
chicken	manók
duck	pato/bibe
turkey	pabo

Animals

cat	pusà
cow	baka
deer	usá
dog	aso
elephant	elepante
goat	kambíng
horse	kabayo
lion	liyón
monkey	unggóy
pig	baboy
sheep	tupa
tiger	tigre
water buffalo	kalabáw

IN THE COUNTRY

DID YOU KNOW ... The best time to travel to the Philippines is from December to May. While it may rain in some places in December and January, the rainy season begins in earnest in June.

Insects, Reptiles & Others

cricket	kuliglíg
cockroach	ípis
crocodile	buwaya
fish	isdâ
fly	langaw
frog	palakâ
leech	lintà
lizard	butikî
mosquito	lamók
snake	ahas
spider	gagambá

FLORA & AGRICULTURE

agriculture	pagsasaka
coconut palm	punò ng niyóg
corn	maís
crops	pananím
flower	bulaklák
harvest (verb)	ani
irrigation	patubig
leaf	dahon
planting/sowing	pagtataním/paghahasík
rice field	palayán
sugar cane	tubó
terraced land	baíbaítang na lupa
tobacco	tabako
tree	punong-kahoy

CROSSWORD – IN THE COUNTRY

Across

2. Optical device for both eyes
5. Disney chose Jiminy to represent this insect
7. Tools for keeping tents upright
8. Wettest season of the year
10. Vital kitchen apparatus
11. Domesticated but notoriously slobby animal

Down

1. Animal with the largest ears
3. Vegetative reproductive system
4. Vertical part of a river
6. Can't see this for the trees
9. Helps you find your way

HEALTH

AT THE DOCTOR

Filipino doctors and dentists speak and understand English, even those in the rural areas.

Where's the ...?	Násaán hô ang ...?
chemist	botíka
dentist	dentista
doctor	doktór
hospital	ospitál

I'm sick.	May sakít hô akó.
My friend is sick.	May sakit hô ang kasama ko.
I need a doctor who speaks English.	Kailangan ko hô ng doktór na marúnong mag-Inglés.

It hurts there.	Masakít hô diyán.
I feel nauseous.	Naalibádbarán/Nasúsuká hô akó.

I've been vomiting.	Nagsúsusuká hô akó.
I feel better/worse.	Mabuti na hô/Mas masamâ hô ang pakiramdam ko.

herbalist	albularyo

AILMENTS

I'm ill.	May sakít hô akó.
I've been vomiting.	Nagsúsusuká hô akó.
I feel under the weather.	Masamâ hô ang pakiramdám ko.
I feel nauseous.	Naáalibádbarán hô akó.
I can't sleep.	Hindi hô akó nakakatulog.

HEALTH

I feel ...	... hô akó.
dizzy	nahihilo
shivery	giníginác
weak	nanghíhinà

I have ...	May ... hô akó.
an allergy	alerdyi
anaemia	anémya
a burn	pasò
cancer	kanser
a cold	sipón
constipation	tibí
cystitis	impeksyón sa dáanan ng ihì
a cough	ubó
influenza	trangkaso
diarrhoea	kursó
a fever	lagnát
a slight fever	sinat
gastroenteritis	impeksyón sa sikmurà
indigestion	impatso
an infection	impeksyón
lice	kuto
a migraine	matinding sakít ng ulo
a pain	sakít
a sprain	pilay
sunburn	sunburn/sunog ng araw sa balat
thrush	singáw
rash	butlíg
lump	bukol
a urinary infection	impeksyón sa pantóg
venereal disease	sakít sa babae
rheumatism	rayuma
worms	bulate

I have a toothache.	Masakít hô ang ngipin ko.
I have a headache.	Masakít hô ang ulo ko.
I have a sore throat.	Masakít hô ang lalamunan ko.
I have a stomachache.	Masakít hô ang tiyán ko.
I have a very sore back.	Masakít na masakít hô ang likód ko.
I have blurred vision.	Nanlalabò hô ang paningín ko.
I have high blood pressure.	Mataás hô ang presyón ko.
I have a heart condition.	May sakít hô akó sa pusò.
I had a relapse.	Nabinat hô akó.

HEALTH

USEFUL PHRASES

I feel better.	Mabuti na hô ang pakiramdam ko.
I feel worse.	Más masamâ hô ang pakiramdam ko.
This is my usual medicine.	Itóng gamót na itó hô ang karaniwan kong iníinóm.
I've been vaccinated.	Nábakunahan na hô akó.
I don't want a blood transfusion.	Ayoko hong magpasalin ng dugô.
Can I have a receipt for my insurance?	Máaarì hô bang makahingî ng resibo para sa insyurans ko?

HEALTH

WOMEN'S HEALTH

Could I see a female doctor?	Puwede hong magpatingin sa babáeng doktór?
I'm pregnant.	Buntís hô akó.
I think I'm pregnant.	Palagáy ko hô buntís akó.
I haven't had my period for ... weeks.	... linggó na hô akong hindî nagkakaregla.
I'm on the pill.	Nagpi-pills hô akó.
I'd like to get the morning-after pill.	Gústo ko hô ng tabletang iniinom sa umaga pagkatapós magtalik.
I'd like to use contraception.	Gústo ko hong gumamit ng pampigil sa pagbubuntís.

abortion	pagpapalaglág
cystic fibrosis	cystic fibriosis
cystitis	impeksyón sa dáanan ng ihì
diaphragm	diaphragm
IUD	IUD
mammogram	X-ray sa suso
menstruation	regla
miscarriage	pagkalaglág
pap smear	pap smear
period pain	
pananakít ng tiyán kapág may regla	
the pill	
pill	
premenstrual tension	
nerbyos bago datnán ng regla	
thrush	
singáw	
ultrasound	
ultrasound	

THEY MAY SAY ...

Buntis ba kayó?;
Nagdadalantáo ba kayó?
    Are you pregnant?
Rinéregla ba kayó?
    Are you menstruating?

SPECIAL HEALTH NEEDS

I'm ...	May ... akó.
diabetic	diabitis
asthmatic	hikà
anaemic	anemya
I'm allergic to antibiotics/ penicillin.	Alerdyik akó sa antibiyotiká/ penisilín.
antibiotics	antibiyotiká
aspirin	aspirina
dairy products	pagkaing gawâ sa gatas
penicillin	penisilín
pollen	pulbín/similyang pulbós ng bulaklák
I have a skin allergy.	May álerdyi ang aking balát.
I've had my vaccinations.	Nagpabakuna na akó.
I have my own syringe.	May sariling hiringgilya akó.
I'm on medication for ...	Umiinóm akó ng gamót para sa ...
I need a new pair of glasses.	Kailangan ko ng bagong salamín.

addiction	sugapà
bite	kagát
blood test	pagsurì ng dugô
contraceptive	pampigil ng pagbubuntís
injection	ineksiyón
injury	kapinsalaan
vitamins	bitamína
wound	sugat

HEALTH

THE DOCTOR MAY SAY ...

Anóng problema?	What's the matter?
Nakakaramdam bá kayó nang anumáng pananakít?	Do you feel any pain?
Saan sumásakít?	Where does it hurt?
Linálagnát ba kayó?	Do you have a temperature?
Gaano katagál na ba kayóng ganitó?	How long have you been like this?
Nagkaroón na ba kayó nitó dati?	Have you had this before?
Meron ba kayóng iníinóm na gamót?	Are you on medication?
Naninigarilyo ba kayó?	Do you smoke?
Umíinóm ba kayó ng alak?	Do you drink?
Nagda-drugs ba kayó?	Do you take drugs?
Alerdyík ba kayó sa anumán?	Are you allergic to anything?
Kelan kayó hulíng nagpatingín sa doktór?	When were you last seen by a doctor?
Kailangan kong tignán iyán ulit.	I'll have to check that again.
Titignán ko ang presyón ng dugô niyó.	Let me check your blood pressure.
Eto ang reseta niyó.	Here's your prescription.

PARTS OF THE BODY

ankle	bukung-bukong	knee	tuhod
		legs	bintî
arm	bráso	liver	atáy
back	likód	lungs	baga
bladder	pantóg	mouth	bibíg
blood	dugô	muscle	lamán/
breasts	suso		kalamanan
buttocks	puwít	nails	kukó
bone	butó	penis	arì ng lalake
chest	dibdíb	ribs	tadyáng
ears	tenga	shoulder	balikat
elbow	siko	skin	balát
eye	matá	stomach	tiyán
finger	dalirì	spleen	palî
fingernail	kukó sa dalirì	teeth	ngipin/ipin
foot	paá	testicles	bayág
hand	kamáy	thigh	hità
hair	buhók	throat	lalamunan
head	ulo	toenail	kukó sa paá
heart	pusò	vagina	arì ng babae
intestines	bituka	vein	ugát
kidney	bató		

HEALTH

DID YOU KNOW ... It's said that no other country has as many beauty contests as the Philippines. Beauty contests are big events and beauty queens are respected, admired and feted as celebrities wherever they go.

HEALTH

AT THE CHEMIST

I need something for ...	Kailangan ko hô ng gamót para sa ...
Do I need a prescription for ...?	Kailangan ko hô ba ng reseta para makabilí ng ...?
How many times a day?	Ilán beses hô sa isáng araw?

antibiotics	antibiyotika
antiseptic	antiseptiko
aspirin	aspirina
bandage	benda
Band-aids	koritas
condoms	kondom
contraceptives	pampigil ng pagbuntis
cotton balls	bulak
cough medicine	gamót sa ubó
gauze	gasa
laxatives	gamót pampurgá
painkillers	gamót na pangpakalma ng kirót
rubbing alcohol	alkohól na panghaplós
sleeping pills	tableta na pampatulog

AT THE DENTIST

HEALTH

I have a toothache.	Masakít hô ang ngipin ko.
I have a hole.	May butas hô akó sa ngipin.
I've lost a filling.	Natanggál hô ang pasta ng ngipin ko.
I've broken my tooth.	Nabalì hô ang ngipin ko.
My gums hurt.	Masakít hô ang gilagid ko.
I don't want it extracted.	Ayoko hong ipabunot yán.
Please give me an anaesthetic.	Lagyán niyó ngâ ng pampamanhíd.
How much is it to have ... ?	Magkano hô ... ?
a tooth filled	magpapasta
a tooth extracted	magpabunot
general cleaning	magpalinis ng lahát ng ngipin
Ouch!	Aray!

CROSSWORD – HEALTH

HEALTH

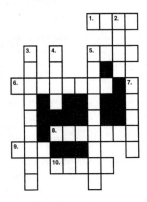

Across

1. Opposite of Delhi Belly and Montezuma's Revenge
5. Hair-infesting creature from the evil world of insects
6. Feeling like reeling
8. What you have when you eat too much
9. Part of body furthest from head
10. Absorbent white clumps of plant fibre

Down

2. Human organ where stones can grow
3. Two epidemics of this virus were called Spanish and Asian
4. Biting, chewing and grinding gear
5. Prominent feature of Lundgren, Van Damme and Stallone
7. Bump

SPECIFIC NEEDS

DISABLED TRAVELLERS

The phrases below are in the polite form.

I'm disabled/handicapped.	May kapansanan/ kapinsalaan hô akó.
I need assistance.	Kailangan ko hô ng tulong.
What services do you have for disabled people?	Anó hô ang mga serbisyo ninyó para sa mga taong may kapansanan?
Is there wheelchair access?	May dáanan hô ba para sa silyang de gulóng?
I'm deaf. Speak more loudly, please.	Bingí akó. Magsalita nga kayó nang mas malakás.
I can lipread.	Nakákabasa akó ng labì.
I have a hearing aid.	May gamit hô akóng hearing aid.
Does anyone here know sign language?	Meron hô ba ditong marunong mag-senyas sa kamáy?
Are guide dogs permitted?	Pinapayagan hô ba ang asong tagá-akay?
braille library	aklatan para sa Braille
disabled person	taong may kapansanan/ kapinsalaan
guide dog	asong tagá-akay
wheelchair	silyang de gulóng

SPECIFIC NEEDS

GAY TRAVELLERS

Gays in the Philippines are active members in the community, participating nationally in political, economic and cultural issues.

The phrases here are in the informal form.

Where are the gay hangouts?	Saán ba dito umiistambay ang mgá gay?
Is there a predominantly gay street/district?	Meron bang kalye/distrito kung saán nakararami ang mgá gay?
Are we/Am I likely to be harassed (here)?	Malamáng kayâ na guluhín akó/kamí (dito)?
Is there a gay bookshop around here?	Meron bang tindahan ng libro para sa mgá gay na malapit dito?
Is there a local gay guide?	Meron bang local gay guide?
Where can I buy some gay/lesbian magazines?	Saán akó makakabilí ng mga mágasín para sa mgá gay/lesbyana?
Is there a gay telephone hotline?	Meron bang telephone hotline para sa mgá gay?

TRAVELLING WITH THE FAMILY

The phrases below are in the polite form.

Are there facilities for babies?	Meron hô bang mgá kagamitán para sa mgá sanggól?
Are children allowed?	Tinatanggap hô ba ang mgá batà?

Do you have a child minding service?	Meron hô bang serbisyo para sa pagbabantay ng mgá batà?
Where can I find a (English-speaking) babysitter?	Saán hô akó makákahanap ng tagá-alagà ng batà na marunong mag-Inglés?
Can you put an (extra) bed/cot in the room?	Máaarì hô bang magdagdag ng kama/tiheras sa kuwarto?
I need a car with a child seat.	Kailangan ko hô ng awto na may úpuan ng batà.
Is it suitable for children?	Angkóp hô ba iyón para sa mgá batà?
Are there any activities for children?	Meron hô bang mga gawain para sa mgá batà?
Is there a family discount?	May tawad hô ba ang pamilya?
Do you have a children's menu?	Meron ba kayóng menúng pambatà?

SPECIFIC NEEDS

DID YOU KNOW ... Perhaps the most famous Filipino author is Dr. Jose Rizal – the Philippine national hero. His books were banned by the Spanish colonisers. He also formed many anti-colonial political movements and when the Philippine revolution broke out in 1896 he was condemned to death for inciting public revolt. He was executed by firing squad on the 30th December 1896 at what is now known as Rizal Park in Manila.

SPECIFIC NEEDS

ON BUSINESS

The phrases below are in the polite form.

We're attending a ...	Dumádaló hô kamí sa isáng ...
conference	kumperensiya
meeting	miting
trade fair	trade fair

I'm on a course.	Nag-aaral hô akó.
I have an appointment with ...	May tipanan hô akó kay ...
Here's my business card.	Eto hô ang business card ko.
I need an interpreter.	Kailangan ko hô ng tagapagsalin.
I need to use a computer.	Kailangan ko hong gumamit ng computer.
I need to send a fax/an email.	Kailangan ko hong mag-fax/ mag-email.

Useful Words

cellular/mobile phone
  cellular phone
client
  kliyente
colleague
  kasamahán
distributor
  tagapamahagì
email
  email
exhibition
  tanghalan

manager	manedyer/tagapamahalà
profit	tubò
proposal	panukalà

K AFTER B

The letter k is pronounced as the 'k' in 'king'.

However, unlike in the English alphabet, the letter k comes straight after the letter b in the Pilipino alphabet.

ON TOUR

These phrases are in the informal form.

We're part of a group.	Kasama kamí ng isáng grupo.
We're on tour.	Nagtu-tour kamí.

I'm with the ...	Miyembro akó ng ...
group	grupo
band	banda
team	koponan
crew	pangkát

Please speak with our manager.	Pakíkausap na lang ang aming manedyer.
We've lost our equipment.	Nawalâ namin ang aming kagamitán.

We sent equipment on this ...	Pinadalá namin ang aming kagamitán sa ... na itó.
flight	flight
train	tren
bus	bus

We're taking a break of ... days.	Magpápahingá kamí ng ... araw.
We're playing on ...	Magtatanghal kamí sa ...

SPECIFIC NEEDS

Film & TV Crews

The phrases below are in the informal form.

We're on location.	On location kamí.
We're filming!	Gumagawâ kamí ng pelíkulá!
May we film here?	Puwede ba kamíng gumawâ ng pelíkulá dito?

We're making a ...	Gumágawâ kamí ng ...
film	pelíkulá
documentary	dokumentáryo
TV series	series sa telebisyón

PILGRIMAGE & RELIGION

What's your religion?	Ano hô ang relihiyón niyó?
I'm not religious.	Hindî akó relihiyóso.
I'm ...	... hô akó.
Buddhist	budista
Christian	kristiyáno

It's worth noting that the Tagalog terms for Hindu, Muslim and
Jewish are considered to be derogatory. It is, on the other hand,
quite acceptable to use the English terms. Most people will
understand these.

Can I attend this service/mass?	Máaari ho bang dumalo sa kultong/misang itó?
Can I pray here?	Puwede ho ba akóng magdasal dito?
Where can I pray/worship?	Saán hô akó máaaring magdasal/sumamba?
Where can I make confession (in English)?	Saán hô akó puwedeng mangumpisál (sa wikang Inglés)?
Can I receive communion here?	Máaari hô ba akóng mangumunyón dito?

baptism/christening	binyág/pagbibinyág
church	simbahan
communion	komunyón
confession	kumpisál
funeral	libíng
prayer	panalangin
priest	parì
relic	relikya
religious procession	prusisyóng pangrelihiyón
sabbath	araw na pangiling
sacraments	mgá sakramento
saint	santo
shrine	dambanà

SPECIFIC NEEDS

TRACING ROOTS & HISTORY

(I think) my ancestors came from this area.	Palagáy ko hô galing dito sa poók na itó ang mgá ninunò ko.
I'm looking for my relatives.	Hinahanap ko hô ang aking mgá kamág-anak.
Is there anyone here by the name of ...?	Meron hô ba ditong taong nagngangalang ...?
I have/had a relative who lived around here.	Meron hô akóng kamág-anak na natirá dito.
	Dati meron hô akong kamág-anak na natirá dito.
I think he fought/died near here.	Lumaban/Namatáy hô yatà siyá malapit dito.
My (father) fought/died here in WW II.	Lumaban/Namatáy hô ang (tatay) ko dito noóng ikalawáng pandáigdigang digmaan.

SPECIFIC NEEDS

My (grandmother) nursed here in WW II.	Nars ang (lola) ko dito noóng ikalawáng pandáigdigang digmaan.
It is in this island that Ferdinand Magellan was killed by Lapu-lapu.	Dito hô sa islang itó pinatay ni Lapu-lapu si Ferdinand Magellan.
This is the monument of José Rizál, the national hero of the Philippines.	Eto hô ang monumento ni José Rizál, ang pambansang bayani ng Pilipinas.

TIME, DATES & FESTIVALS

TELLING THE TIME

Spanish numbers (with Tagalog spellings) are commonly used to tell the time.

What time is it?	Anóng oras na?
It's (five) o'clock. (am)	Alás (singko) na ng umaga. Ika-(limá) na ng umaga.
It's (seven) o'clock. (pm)	Alás (siyete) na ng gabí. Ika-(pitó) na ng gabí.

'Half past' is expressed by the word imédya:

It's half past (six).	Alás (seis) imedya. Kalahating oras makalipas ang ika-(anim). Tatlumpung sandalî makalipas ang ika-(anim).
It's half past (eight).	Alas (otso) imedya. Kalahting oras makalipas ang ika-(waló). Tatlumpúng minuto makalipas ang ika-(waló).

Times can be expressed as so many minutes past the hour:

(Nine) fifteen.	Alas (nuwebe) kinse; Labinlimáng sandali makalipas ang ika-(siyám).

Times can also be expressed as the next hour minus (**menos**) so many minutes.

Quarter to two.	**Ménos kínse pára alas síngko.**
	Labinlimáng sandalí bago mag-ikalawá.

The Pilipino counterparts of 'am' and 'pm' are: **n.u.** (**ng umaga** – in the morning), **n.t.** (**ng tanghalì**– at noon), **n.h.** (**ng hapon** – in the afternoon) **n.g.** (**ng gabí** – in the evening/at night)

DAYS OF THE WEEK

Monday	**Lunes**
Tuesday	**Martes**
Wednesday	**Miyérkolés**
Thursday	**Huwebes**
Friday	**Biyernes**
Saturday	**Sábado**
Sunday	**Linggó**

MONTHS

January	**Enero**
February	**Pebrero**
March	**Marso**
April	**Abríl**
May	**Mayo**
June	**Hunyo**
July	**Hulyo**
August	**Agosto**
September	**Setyembre**
October	**Oktubre**
November	**Nobyembre**
December	**Disyembre**

TIME, DATES & FESTIVALS

DATES

What date is it today?	Anóng pétsa ngayón?
It's the (24th of February).	Ngayón ay (abeynte kuwatro ng Pebrero).
	Ngayón ay (ikádawampú't apat ng Pebrero).

PRESENT

today	ngayóng araw
this morning	ngayóng umaga
today at noontime	ngayóng tanghalì
this afternoon	ngayóng hapon
today at midnight	ngayóng hátinggabí
tonight	ngayóng gabí
this week	ngayóng linggó
this month	ngayóng buwán
this year	ngayóng taón
now	ngayón
right now	ngayón mismo

TIME, DATES & FESTIVALS

DID YOU KNOW ... The Philippines is the only country in Asia in which Christians are in the majority. Over 90% of Filipinos are Christian with 80% being Roman Catholic. About 8% of the population is Muslim.

TIME, DATES & FESTIVALS

PAST

yesterday	kahapon
day before yesterday	kamakalawá/noóng isang araw
yesterday morning	kahapon ng umaga
last night	kagabí
last week	noóng isáng linggó
last month	noóng isang buwán
last year	noóng isáng taón
half an hour ago	kalahating oras na ang nakalipas
a while ago	kanina
last Friday	noóng Biyernes
since May	buhat noóng Mayo

FUTURE

tomorrow	bukas
day after tomorrow	samakalawá/sa isáng bukas
tomorrow morning	bukas ng umaga
tomorrow afternoon	bukas ng hapon
tomorrow evening	bukas ng gabí
later (in the day)	mamayâ
tonight	ngayóng gabí
next week	sa isáng linggó
next month	sa isáng buwán
next year	sa isáng taón
in (eight) days	sa loób ng (waló)-ng araw
in September	sa Setyembre
on Saturday	sa Linggó

DURING THE DAY

afternoon	hápon
dawn	madalíng araw
day	araw
early	maaga
midnight	hatinggabí
morning	umaga
night	gabí
noon	tangháli
sunrise	pagsikat ng araw
sunset	paglubóg ng araw

FESTIVALS
Christmas & New Year
The Christmas season in the Philippines extends up to the feast of the Epiphany (6th January), although Christmas itself is celebrated on the traditional December 25th.

Christmas Traditions
The Christmas season is a very happy season in the Philippines. It's a season when families and friends come together to celebrate. You can feel the Christmas spirit as early as the second week of December. By this time, people are starting to put up their Christmas decorations and to hang their colourful **paról** (Christmas lanterns). Much like in many countries, Christmas has become very commercialised, though many locals say that they feel the true spirit of Christmas of giving, forgiving and loving has remained.

Early morning masses start from the 15th of December and culminate on the 24th of December, when the **simbang gabi** (midnight mass) is held. The midnight mass is very well attended and almost all churches will be filled to capacity. After the midnight mass, the family goes home to have their noche buena (midnight Christmas feast). In most families, it is after the noche buena that gifts are exchanged.

Christmas day is the time for receiving visitors, usually relatives and friends. Parents take their children to their ninongs (god-fathers) and ninangs (godmothers), who give them their Christmas presents.

New Year Traditions

Filipinos celebrate the New Year very noisily. You can hear fire-crackers even as early as the second week of December, when the Christmas season starts. By New Year's Eve, the 31st of December, the noise of the firecrackers reaches a crescendo pretty much like that of a full blown war. At midnight the noise peaks, and anyone who experiences this for the first time will surely be amazed. The sky is alit with all sorts of pyrotechnic displays.

Easter

The Easter season in the Philippines, a predominantly Catholic country, is a solemn religious period. It starts on 'Ash Wednesday'. Shops, offices and schools are closed on 'Maundy Thursday' and 'Good Friday'. Early morning masses are held in the churches on Easter.

Town Fiestas

Town fiestas are held to celebrate the feasts of saints. They go on the whole day and every family prepares food for everyone, even strangers.

Historical Events

'Independence Day', the commemoration of the granting of in-dependence to the Philippines by Spain, is held on the 12th of June and is a national holiday.

FESTIVE EXPRESSIONS

Merry Christmas!	Maligayang Paskó!
Happy New Year!	Maligayang Bagong Taón!
Merry Christmas and a Prosperous New Year!	Maligayang Paskó at Manigong Bagong Taon!
Best wishes!	Maligayang Batì!
Happy Birthday!	Maligayang Batì sa inyóng Kaarawán! (pol)
	Maligayang Batì sa iyóng Kaarawán! (inf)
My condolences.	Nakikiramay akó. (inf)
	Nakikiramay hô akó. (pol)

Celebrations

Parties are usually held for birthdays, christenings, weddings, graduations from the university or promotions at work. When a person dies, after the funeral services, prayers are held every evening for nine consecutive days at the home of the family. On the ninth day, the people participating in the novena get together and partake of the party food served at the table.

Some Useful Words

Christmas	paskó
Christmas Eve	bisperás ng paskó
Christmas lantern	paról
New Year	bagóng taon
New Year's Eve	bisperás ng bagong taón
Holy Week	Mahal na Araw; Semana Santa
Easter	Linggó ng Pagkabuhay

CROSSWORD – TIME, DATES & FESTIVALS

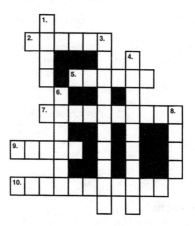

TIME, DATES & FESTIVALS

Across

2. Probably the last time you slept
5. This very moment
7. Happy birthday Jesus! (second word)
9. The month with the letter 'i'
10. Holiest week of the year

Down

1. The year of today (second word)
3. Three days ahead of yesterday (last two words)
4. The ninth month, once upon a time
6. More than a little while ago
8. Sunless hours

NUMBERS

There are two sets of numbers: the native Pilipino, and the Spanish, written the Pilipino way. Spanish numbers are used for times, dates, with prices which have both the high and low denominations or are above 10 pesos. English numbers are also widely used to express prices. For example the price 'P 1.50' is **uno singkuwenta** or **one fifty**, but 'P1.00' is simply **piso** in Pilipino.

CARDINAL NUMBERS

	Spanish	Pilipino
1	uno	isá
2	dos	dalawá
3	tres	tatló
4	kuwatro	apat
5	singko	limá
6	seis	anim
7	siyete	pitó
8	otso	waló
9	nuwebe	siyám
10	diyes	sampû
11	onse	labíng-isá
12	dose	labíndalawá
13	trése	labíntatló
14	katórse	labíng-ápat
15	kínse	labínlimá
16	disiseis	labíng-ánim
17	disisiyete	labímpitó
18	disiotso	labíng-waló
19	disinuwebe	labínsiyám
20	beynte	dalawampû
21	beynte uno	dalawampu't isá
22	beynte dos	dalawampu't dalawá

30	treynta	tatlumpû
40	kuwarenta	ápatnapû
50	singkuwenta	limampû
60	sisenta	ánimnapû
70	sitenta	pitumpû
80	otsénta	walumpû
90	nobenta	siyamnapû
100	siyento	sandaán
1000	isang mil	isáng libo; sanlibo
one million	isang milyon	isáng angaw

ORDINAL NUMBERS

1st	úna	6th	ikaánim
2nd	ikalawá	7th	ikapitó
3rd	ikatló	8th	ikawaló
4th	ikaápat	9th	ikasiyám
5th	ikalimá	10th	ikasampû

FRACTIONS

Except for the fraction kalahatì (a half or 1/2) the other fractions in Pilipino are seldom used. The English fractions are used instead.

USEFUL WORDS

percent	bahagdán	once	isáng beses
a dozen	isáng dosena	twice	dalawáng
a pair	isáng pares		beses

NUMBERS

EMERGENCIES

Help!	Saklolo!
Stop!	Tumigil ka!
Go away!	Umalís ka!
Thief!	Magnanakáw!
Fire!	Sunog!
Watch out!	Ingat!
Call the police!	Tumawag ka ng pulís!
Call a doctor!	Tumawag ka ng doktór!
Call an ambulance!	Tumawag ka ng ambulansiya!
I've been robbed.	Ninakawan akó!
I've been bashed.	Binugbóg akó.
I've been raped.	Ginahasà akó!
I am ill.	May sakít akó.
My friend is ill.	May sakít ang kasama ko.
I have medical insurance.	May insyurans akó na magbabayad ng aking págpapagamót.
I'm lost.	Nawawalâ akó.
I've lost my ...	Nawalán akó ng ...
bags	bagahe/mgá daládalahan
money	pera
travellers' cheques	travellers' check
passport	pasport
My possessions are insured.	Nakasiguro ang aking mgá gamit.

EMERGENCIES

Where are the toilets?	Násaán hô ang CR?
I'm sorry/I apologise.	Sori hô.
I didn't realise I was doing anything wrong.	Hindî ko alám na may nágawâ palá akóng malî.
I didn't do it.	Hindî ko iyón ginawâ.
I wish to contact my embassy/ consulate.	Gústo kong tawagan ang embahada/konsuládo ko.

The influence of Spanish and, more recently, English on Pilipino is quite apparent in the words included here. These words are spelled the way Pilpinos would pronounce them. You'll notice that in conversing, Filipinos, particularly from Manila, use a lot of English words and phrases, especially for articles and concepts, both old and new, which are of western origin. Some examples of these words are cassette, CD, cross country trail, surfboard, mountain bike, cable TV, contact lenses, computer, homeopathy, aromatherapy, etc. There are also some English terms – medical, travel and sport, among others, which are currently so commonly used that it has become clear that there is no need to devise Pilipino counterparts for them. Such words have not been included in the vocabulary list.

English entries in the list which may have no single-word counterparts in Pilipino have been paraphrased. English words more commonly used than their Pilipino counterparts have been given in English in some of the phrases.

A

able (to be); can	máaarì/puwede

Can (may) I take your photo?
Máaarì ko ba kayóng kunan ng litrato? (pol)
Can you show me on the map?
Puwede mo bang ipakita sa akin sa mapa? (inf)

aboard	nakasakáy
abortion	pagpapalaglág
above	sa itaás
abroad	nasa ibáng bansa
to accept	tanggapín
accident	aksidente/sakunâ
accommodation	túluyan
across	sa kabilâ
activist	aktibista
acid (drug)	ásidó/LSD
addiction	sugapà
address	tírahan
to admire	humangà
admission	pagpapasok
to admit	papasukin
adult	nasa gulang
advantage	kabutihan
advice	payò

A

aeroplane	eroplano
to be afraid of	takót sa
after	pagkatapos
[in the] afternoon (1-5 pm)	[ng] hapon
this afternoon	ngayóng hapon
again	ulî/mulî
against	laban sa
age	gulang/edád
aggressive	basag-ulero
a while ago	kanina
[half an hour] ago	[kalahating oras] na ang nakalipas
to agree	sumáng-ayon
I don't agree.	Hindî ako sang-ayon.
Agreed!	Ayós!
agriculture	pagsasaka
ahead	una/náuuná
aid (help)	tulong
air	hangin
air-conditioned	may erkon
air mail	koreong pang-himpapawíd
airport	páliparan
alarm clock	relő na may-panggising
all	lahát
allergy	alérhiya/álerdyi
to allow	pumayag
almost	halos

alone	mag-isá
already	na
also	din/rin
altar	altár/dambanà
altitude	taás/tayog
always	lagì
amateur	baguhan/ di propesyunál
ambassador	embahadór (m)/ embahadora (f)
among	sa mgá
anarchist	anarkista
ancient	ng unang panahón
and	at
anaemia	anemya
anger	galit
angry	galit
animals	mgá hayop
ankle	bukong-bukong
annual	táunan
answer	sagót
ant	langgám
antenna	antena
anthologies	mgá antolohiya
antibiotics	mgá antibiyotiko
anti-nuclear group	grupong anti-nuclear
antiques	mgá antigo
antiseptic	pandisimpekta
any	kahit/maskí anó
appendix	apendiks
April	Abríl
appointment	típanan

English	Pilipino
architect	arkitekto
architecture	arkitektura
to argue	magtalo
arm	braso
to arrive	dumating
arrivals	mgá pagdatíng
art	sining
art gallery	galeriya
artist	artista
ashtray	sinisero
to ask (for something)	humingî
to ask (a question)	magtanóng
aspirin	aspirina
athletic	atletiks/ pálakasan
asthmatic	híkain
atmosphere	alangaang
aunt	tiya
autumn	taglagás
avenue	abenida
awful	nakakatakot

B

English	Pilipino
baby	batà
baby food	pagkain ng batà
baby powder	pulbós pambatà
babysitter	yayà
back (body)	likód
at the back	sa likurán
bad	masamâ

English	Pilipino
badge	tsapa
bag	supot (paper)/ bayóng (made of woven palm leaves)
baggage	daládalahan/ bagahe
bakery	panaderyá
balcony	balkón/ balkonahe
ballet	baléy
ball	bola
band (music)	banda
bandage	benda
bank	bangko
banknotes	kuwartáng papél
baptism	binyág
baseball	beysbol
basketball	basketbol
bath	paliligô
basket	basket
bathing suit	damit-pampaligô
bathroom	banyo/ páliguan
battery	batiryá
to be	

(Note: Pilipino has no verb 'to be', in some instances, the particle ay takes the function of 'to be' – see Grammar chapter page 33.)

English	Pilipino
beach	tabíng-dagat/ aplaya
beak	tukâ
bear	oso
beautiful	magandá

B

because	dahil/kasí
bed	kama
bedbug	surot
bedroom	kuwartong-tulugán
before	noón/dati
beggar	pulubi
begin	magumpisá/magsimulâ
behind	sa likurán
below	nasa/sa babâ
beside	nasa/sa tabí
best	pinakamagalíng
a bet	tayâ/pustá
between	nasa/sa pagitan
the Bible	ang Bibiliyá
bicycle/bike	bisikleta
big	malakí
bill	kuwenta
billiards	bilyár
binoculars	largabista
biography	talámbuhay/biyograpiya
bird	ibon

birth certificate
katibayan ng pagsilang/
sertipiko ng pagsilang

birthday	kaarawán
bite (dog, insect)	kagát
black	itím
B&W (film)	waláng kulay
blanket	blangket
to bleed	magdugô
to bless	basbasán/bendisyunán

Bless you!
Susmaryosep!
(An expression used by the older
generation which is hardly used
now. It is actually the contracted
form of Hesús, Mariá, Hosép or
Jesus, Mary, Joseph.)

blind	bulág
blister	paltós
blood	dugó
blood group	urì ng dugó
blood pressure	presyón ng dugô

high blood pressure
mataás na presyón ng dugô
low blood pressure
mababang presyón ng dugô

blood test	pagsusurì sa dugô
blue	asúl/bugháw
to board (ship)	sumakáy
boat	bapór/bangká (a smaller native boat)
body	katawán

Let's start eating!/Bon appétit!
Magumpisá na tayo!
Bon voyage!
Maligayang paglakbay!

bone	butó
book	libró/aklát
to book	magreserba
bookshop	tindahan ng libró
boots	botas

border	hangganan
bored	naíiníp
boring	nakakaantók/ nakákainíp
to borrow	humirám
both	kapwà/pareho
bottle	bote/botelya
bottle opener	pambukás ng bote/botelya
[at the] bottom	[nasa/sa] ibabâ
box	kahón
boxing	boksing
boy	batang lalaki
boyfriend	nobyo
branch	sangáy
of brass	yarì sa tansô
brave	matapang
bread	tinapay
to break	masirà
broken	sirâ
breakfast	almusál/ agahan
breast	dibdíb
breasts	suso
to breathe	humingá
a bribe	suhol/lagáy/ pabagsák (col)
to bribe	magsuhol/ maglagáy/ magpabagsák (col)
bridge	tuláy
brilliant	matalino
to bring	dalhín
broken (glass)	baság
brother	kapatíd na lalaki

brown	kayumanggî/ kulay-kapé
a bruise	pasâ
bucket	timbâ/baldé
Buddhist	budista
to build	magtayô
building	gusalì
bum/ass	puwít
a burn	pasò
bus (city)	bus
bus (intercity)	bus na pampro- binsiya
business	negosyo
business person	negosyante/ komersyante/ mangangalakal
bus station	istasyón ng bus
bus stop	hintuan ng bus
busy	abalá
but	pero
butterfly	paruparó
buttons	mga butones
to buy	bumilí

I'd like to buy ...
Gústo kong bumilí... (inf)
Where can I buy a ticket?
Saán akó puwedeng bumilí ng tiket? (inf)

C

cake shop	bakeshop (English)
calendar	kalendaryo

C

camera	kámerá
camera shop	tindahan ng kamerá
to camp	magkampo
Can we camp here?	
Puwede ba kaming magkampo dito? (pol)	
campsite	lugár ng pagkampohan
can (to be able)	
Note: the prefix ma- or maka- is attached to the root of the verb	
We can do it.	
Magágawâ namin itó. (inf)	
I can't do it.	
Hindî ko hô magágawâ iyán. (pol)	
can (aluminium)	lata
can opener	pambukás ng lata; abre-lata
to cancel	kanselahín
candle	kandilà
canter	yagyág
car	awto/kotse
car owner's title	papeles ng awto
car registration	rehistro ng awto
to care (about)	intindihin
to care (for someone)	mahalín
Careful!	
Ingat lang!	
cards	mga kard
caring	mapágmahál

to carry	kargahín
carton	kartón
cartoons	kartún
cash register	kaha
cashier	kahero (m)/ kahera (f)
castle	kastilyo
cat	pusà
cathedral	katedrál
Catholic	katoliko (m)/ katolika (f)
caves	mga kuweba
to celebrate	ipágdiwang
centimetre	sentimetro
certificate	sertipíko
chair	silya
champagne	sampán
championships	mgá kampeonato
chance	pagkakátaón
to change	magpalít
change (coins)	baryá/suklî
changing rooms	mga kuwartong mapagpápalitán
channel (TV)	istásyon/ himpilan
charming	kaakit-akit
to chat up	umiiskor (slang)
cheap hotel	murang otél; otél na mura
a cheat	mandarayà
Cheat!	
Mandarayà!	
to check	tingnán
cheese	keso
chemist	botika/parmasya

chess	ahedres/tses	cliff	dalisdís
chess board	damahán	to climb	umakyát
chest	dibdíb	cloak	balabal
chicken	manók	clock	reló
child	batà	to close	sarhán
childminding	pagbabantáy ng batà	closed	sarado
		clothing	damít
children	mgá batà	clothing store	tindahan ng damít
chocolate	tsokolate		
to choose	pumilì	cloud	ulap
Christian	kristiyano	cloudy	maulap
christian name	pangalang kristiyano	clown	payaso
		clutch (car)	klats
Christmas Day	araw ng Paskó	coach (trainer)	tagasanay
Christmas Eve	bisperás ng Paskó	coast	baybay
		coat	balabal/ amerikana
church	simbahan		
cigarette papers	mgá papél ng sigarilyo	cockroaches	mgá ipis
		coins	sinsilyo baryá
cigarettes	mgá sigarilyo	a cold	sipón
cinema	sinehán	cold (adj)	malamíg/ magináw
circus	sirko		
citizenship	pagkamámamayán	It's cold.	
city	lungsód/ siyudád	Ang lamíg.	
		to have a cold	may sipón
city centre	sentro ng siyudád	cold water	malamíg na tubig
classical art	sining na klásikó		
		colleague	kasamahán
classical theatre	teatrong klásikó	college	kolehiyo
		colour	kulay
clean	malinis	comb	sukláy
clean hotel	malinis na otél; otél na malinis	to come	pumarito
		to come/arrive	dumatíng
cleaning (n)	ang paglinis	comedy	komedya
client	kliyente	comet	kometa/ buntalà

C

comfortable	maginhawà/komportable
comics	komiks
communion	komunyón
communist	komunista
companion	kasama
company	kumpanyá
compass	kumpas
a concert	konsiyerto
condoms	mgá kondom
confession (religious)	kumpisál
to confirm (a booking)	tiyakín
Congratulations! Maligayang batì!	
conservative	konserbatibo
to be constipated	tinitibí
constipation	tibí
construction work	gawain sa konstruksiyón
consulate	konsulado
contemporary (adj)	ng/sa panahóng itó
contemporary films	mgá pelíkulá ng panahóng itó
contraception	pagpigil ng pagbubuntis
contraceptives	pampigil ng pagbubuntis
contract	kontrata
convent	kumbento
to cook	maglutò
corner	kanto
cork	tapón
corrupt	tiwalí

to cost	magkahalagá
How much does it cost to go to ...? Magkano ang papuntá sa ...? (inf)	
It costs a lot. Mahál na mahál.	
country	probinsiya/lalawigan
countryside	kabukiran
a cough	ubó
to count	bilangin
coupon	kupón
court (legal)	húkúman/korte
court (sports)	láruan
cow	baka
crafts	mgá kasanayan sa paggawà ng mga bagáy sa kamáy
crafty	madayà
crag	nakausling matarik na bató
crazy	balíw; lokó-lokó (m)/loka-loka (f)
cricket (insect)	kuliglíg
cross (religious)	krus
cross (angry)	galit
a cuddle	yakap
cup	tasa
cupboard	paminggalan
curator	tagapamahalà
current affairs	mgá pangkasalukuyang pangyayari

customs — adwana
to cut — putulin
to cycle — magbisikleta
cycling — pagbibisikleta
cyclist — siklista
cystitis — impeksiyón sa daanan ng ihì

D

dad — itáy/papá
daily — araw-araw
dairy products — mgá produktong yarì sa gatas
to dance — magsayáw
dancing (n) — pagsayáw
dangerous — peligroso/mapanganib
dark — madilím
date (appointment) — típanan
date (time) — petsa
to date — makipagtipanan
date of birth — araw ng pagsilang
daughter — anák na babae
dawn — madaling-araw
day — araw
day after tomorrow — samakalawá
day before yesterday — kamakalawá
in (six) days — pagkalipas ng (anim) na araw
dead — patáy
deaf — bingí
to deal — magtindá

death — kamatayan
December — Disyembre
to decide — magpasiyá
deck (of cards) — manghál ng baraha
deep — malalim
deer — usá
deforestation — pagsisirà ng kagubatan
degree — tituló
delay — pagkaatraso
delirious — nahíhibáng
democracy — demokrasya
demonstration — demonstrasyón
dentist — dentista
to deny — magkailâ
deodorant — pang-alís ng amóy
to depart (leave) — umalís
department stores — mgá malalakíng tindahan
departure — pag-alís
descendent — galing sa
desert — disyerto
design — dibuho
destination — paróroonán
to destroy — sirain
detail — detalye
diabetic — diyabétikó
diarrhoea — kursó
diary — taláarawán
dice/die — dais
dictionary — diksiyunaryo
different — ibá
difficult — mahirap
(also the word for 'poor')

dinner	hapunan	double	doble
direct	tuwíran	a double bed	isáng kamang pangdalawahan
director	direktór/ tagapamahalà	a double room	isáng kuwartong pangdalawahan
dirty	marumí/ madumí	a dozen	isáng dosena
disabled	may kapansanan/ kapinsalaán	draughts	dama
		drama	drama
		dramatic	madulâ
disadvantage	disbentaha	to draw	idrowing/iguhit
discount	tawad	to dream	managinip
to discover	matuklasán	dress	barò/bestido
discrimination	pagtatangì	a drink	ínumin
disease	sakit/ karamdaman	to drink	uminóm
		to drive	magmaneho
dismissal	pagpapaalís	driver's licence	lisensiya
distributor	tagapamahagì	drug	gamót
diving (n)	pagsisid	drug addiction	pagkagumon sa bawal na gamót
diving equipment	kagamitán na pangsisid	drug dealer	nagtitindá ng bawal na gamót
dizzy	hiló		
to do	gawín	drugs	mga bawal na gamót
What are you doing?			
Anóng ginágawà mo? (inf)		drums	mga tamból
I didn't do it.		to be drunk	lasíng
Hindî ko hô iyón ginawâ.(pol)		to dry (clothes)	matuyô
doctor	doktór/ manggagamot	dummy (baby's)	tsupón
documentary	dokumentaryo		
dog	aso		
dolls	mga manikà		
door	pintô	**E**	
donkey	buriko	each	bawat
dope (drugs)	mga bawal na gamót	ear	tenga

English	Pilipino
early	maaga
It's early.	
Maaga pa.	
to earn	kumita
earrings	mgá hikaw
ears	mgá tenga
Earth	mundó
earth (soil)	lupà
earthquake	lindól
east	silangan
Easter	Linggó ng Pagkabuhay
easy	madalí
to eat	kumain
economy	ekonomiya/ kabuhayan
editor	patnugot
education	edukasyón
eight	waló
eighteen	labing-waló
eighth	ikawaló
eighty	walumpû
elections	halalan
electorate	mga botante
electricity	elektrisidád/ kuryente
elevator	elebeytor
eleven	labíng-isá
embarassed	mápahiyà
embarassment	pagkápahiyà
embassy	embahada
employee	empleado (m)/ empleada (f)
employer	amo (coll)
empty	waláng-lamán
end	wakás

English	Pilipino
to end	tapusin
endangered species	egá urì ng hayop at taním na nanganganib sa pagkalipol
engagement	kompromiso
engine	mákina
engineer	inhinyero
engineering	inhinyeriya
England	Inglatera
English	Inglés
to enjoy (oneself)	maglibáng
enough	sapát/hustó
Enough!	
Tama na!	
to enter	pumasok
entertaining	nakákaalíw/ nakákalibáng
envelope	sobre
environment	kapaligirán
epileptic	hímatayin
Epiphany	Pistá ng Tatlong Harì/ Epipanya
epoch	panahón
equality	pagkakápantáy-pantáy
equipment	mga kagamitán
erection	pagtayô
etching	disenyong inukit sa metál
european	tagá-yuropa
evening	gabí
every day	araw-araw
example	halimbawà
For example, ...	
Halimbawá, ...	

F

excellent	nápakagalíng
exchange	pálitan
to exchange (money)	magpalít
exchange rate	halagá ng pálitan
excluded	hindî isinama
Excuse/Pardon me.	
Iskyus lang. (inf)	
Iskyus lang hô. (pol)	
to apologise	
Pagpaumanhín hô ninyó.(pol)	
to ask permission to leave	
Paumanhín hô. (pol)	
to ask to speak	
Mawaláng-galang hô. (pol)	
to exhibit	itanghál
exhibition	tanghalan
exit	lábasan
expensive	mahál
exploitation	pagsasamantalá
express	ekspres
express mail	koreong ekspres
eye	matá

F

face	mukhâ
factory	pábriká/ págawaan
factory worker	manggagawà sa pábriká
fall (autumn)	tag-lagás
family	pamilya/ mag-anak
famous	bantóg

fan (hand-held)	pamaypáy/ abaniko
fan (machine)	bentiladór
fans (of a team)	mgá tagahangà (ng isang koponan)
Fantastic!	
Pantástikó!	
far	malayò
farm	bukid
farmer	magsasaka
fast	mabilís
fat	matabá
father	amá/tatay
father-in-law	biyenáng lalaki
fault (in manufacture)	depekto
fault (someone's)	kasalanan
faulty	may-sirà/ may-depekto
fear	takot
February	Pebrero
to feel ...	makaramdam ng ...
feelings	mgá damdamin
fence	bakod
fencing	pagieskrima
festival	piyesta/pistá
fever	lagnát
few	kauntî
fiancé/fiancée	nobyo/nobya
fiction	kathâ
field	parang
fifteen	labinlimá
fifth	ikalimá
fifty	limampú

F

fight	laban
to fight	mag-away
to fight against	lumaban
figures	mgá bilang
to fill	punuín
film (negatives)	negatibo
film (cinema)	pelíkulá
film (for camera)	pilm/pelíkulá
films	pelíkulá/sine
to find	makakita
a fine	multá
finger	dalirí
fire (controlled)	apóy
fire (uncontrolled)	sunog
firewood	kahoy na panggatong
first	una
first aid kit	kahon ng unang panglunas
fish	isdâ
fish shop	tindahan ng isdâ
five	limá
flag	watawat/ bandila
flat (land)	patag
flea	pulgás
flashlight (torch)	lente/plaslayt
flight	paglipád ng eruplano
floor	sahíg
floor (storey)	palapag
flour	arina
flower	bulaklák
flower seller	tindera/o ng bulaklák (f/m)

fly	langaw
It's foggy.	
Maulop.	
to follow	sumunód
food (to take)	take away
foot	paá
football	putbol
footpath	bangketa
foreign	banyaga
forest	gubat
forever	habang-buhay; lagì
to forget	makalimutan
I forget.	
Nakakalimutan ko. (inf)	
Forget about it!;Don't worry!	
Kalimutan mo na iyón!;	
Huwag mong intindihin iyón! (inf)	
to forgive	patawarin
fortnight	kinsena
fortune teller	manghuhulà
forty	apatnapû
four	apat
fourteen	labing-apat
fourth	ikaápat
foyer	bulwagan
free (not bound)	kawalâ/hindi nakatalì
free (of charge)	waláng bayad/ libre
to freeze	magyelo
Friday	Biyernes
friend	kaibigan
It's frosty.	
Nagyeyelo.	

G

frozen foods	mgá eladong pagkain
fruit picking	pamimitás ng prutas
full	punô
fun	sayá
for fun	bilang libangan
to have fun	maglibáng
to make fun of	biruin
funeral	libíng
future	hináharáp

G

game (sport)	larô
garage	talyér (car repair shop)
	garahe (place for keeping cars)
garbage	basura
gardening	paghahardín
gardens	mgá hardín
gas cartridge	tanké ng gas
gate	tárangkahan
gay	binabaé/baklâ; badíng/ sward (col)
gear stick	kambyo
general	panlahát
Get lost!	
Alís dyán!	
gift	regalo/ aginaldo
gig	kalesa/karetela
girl	batang babae

girlfriend	kasintahan na babae/ babaeng kaibigan
to give	bigyán
Could you give me ...?	
Máaarì mo ba akóng bigyán ...? (inf)	
glass	salamín/kristál
to go	pumuntá
Let's go.	
Halina.	
We'd like to go to ...	
Gústo naming pumuntá sa ... (inf)	
Go straight ahead.	
Tulóy-tulóy lang hô. (pol)	
to go out with	lumabás kasama
goal	gol
goat	kambíng
God	Diyós
(made of) gold	(na) gintô
Good afternoon.	
Magandáng hapon.	
Good evening/night.	
Magandáng gabí.	
Good health!/Cheers!	
Mabuhay!	
good hotel	mabuting otél otél na mabuti
Good luck!	
Buwenas!	
Good morning.	
Magandáng umaga.	
Goodbye.	
Paalam.	

English	Pilipino
goose	gansâ
government	pámahalaán/ gobyerno
gram	gramo
grandchild	apó
grandfather	lolo
grandmother	lola
grapes	mgá ubas
grass	damó (also col for marijuana)
grave	puntód/ libingan (n)
great	malakí
Great!	Ang galing!
green	berde
greengrocer	tindahan ng gulay
grey	kulay-abó
to guess	hulaan
guide (person)	giya
guidebook	aklat památnubay
guided trek	paglakád na may giya
guitar	gitara
gym	himnasyo/ dyim
gymnastics	dyimnastiks

H

English	Pilipino
hair	buhók
hairbrush	sipilyong pambuhók
half	kalahati (n)
half a litre	kalahating litro
to hallucinate	magpagunigunî
ham	hamón
hammer	martilyo
hammock	duyan
hand	kamáy
handbag	hanbag
handicrafts	pagyari sa kamáy
handlebars	manibela
handmade	yarí sa kamáy
handsome	guwapo
happy	masayá
Happy birthday!	Maligayang batì sa iyóng káarawán! (inf)
harbour	piyér/daungan
hard	matigás
harness	guwarnasyón
harrassment	pangguguló
hash	mariwana
to have	magkaroón; may/mayroón (See page 33.)
Do you have ...?	Mayroón ba kayóng ...? (pol)
I have ...	Mayroón hô akóng ... (pol)
hayfever	álerdyi sa pulbín
he	siyá
head	ulo
a headache	sakit ng ulo
health	kalusugan
to hear	maríníg
heart	pusô

169

H

heat — init
heater — pampainit
heavy — mabigát
  Hello.
  Kumustá.
  Hello! (answering telephone)
  Helo!
to help — tumulong
  Help!
  Saklolo!
hen — inahíng manók
herbs — mgá damong panggamót
herbalist — albularyo
here — dito
heroin — erowina
heroin addict — sugapà sa erowina
high — mataás
high school — mataás na páaralán
to hike — maglakád nang malayò
hiking — paglakad nang malayò
hiking boots — botas na panglakad nang malayò
hiking routes — mga daán para sa paglakad nang malayò
hill — buról/maliít na bundók
to hire — umupa/umalkilá
  Where can I hire a bicycle?
  Saán akó puwedeng umalkilá ng bisikleta? (inf)

to hitchhike — umangkás
holiday — piyesta/waláng pasok
holidays — bakasyón
Holy Week — Semana Santa; Mahál na Araw
homelessness — pagkalagalág
homosexual — homoseksuwál
honey — pulót-pukyutan
honeymoon — pulót-gatâ
horrible — nakakakilabot/ nakakatakot
horse — kabayo
horse riding — pangangabayo
hospital — ospitál
hot — mainit
  It's hot.
  Mainit.
  It's hot today.
  Mainit ngayóng araw.
  The coffee is hot.
  Mainit ang kapé.
to be hot — mainitan
hot water — mainit na tubig
house — bahay
housework — gawain sa bahay
how — paano
  How do I get to ...?
  Paano ko hô marárating ang ...? (pol)
  How do you say ...?
  Paano sabihin ...? (inf)
hug — yakap/yapós
human rights — karapatáng pantao
a hundred — sandaán

hunger	gutóm
hungry	gutóm
husband	asawa/táo (col)

I

I	akó
ice	yelo
ice axe	palakól na pangyelo
ice cream	sorbetes
identification card	ID (English)
identification	palátandaan
idiot	idyota/tangá
if	kung
ill	may sakít
immigration	imigrasyón/ pandarayuhan
important	mahalagá/ importante

It's important.
Importante iyón. (inf)
It's not important.
Hindi iyón importante. (inf)

in a hurry	apurado
in front of	sa haráp ng
included	kasama
income tax	buwís sa kita
incomprehensible	di-maunawaan
indigestion	impatso
industry	industriya
inequality	di-pagkaká-pantáy-pantáy
to inject	iniksiyunán
injection	iniksiyón
injury	pinsalà
inside	nasa/sa loób

instructor	tagapagturò
insurance	seguro/ insyurans
intense	matindí
interesting	kawili-wili
intermission	pahingá
international	pandaigdig
interview	panayám
island	isla
itch	katí
itinerary	itiniraryo

J

jail	bilangguan/ bilibid
jar	garapón
jealous	seloso (m)/ selosa (f)
jeans	maóng
jeep	dyip
jewellery	alahas
job	trabaho
job advertisement	patalastás
jockey	hinete
joke	birò
to joke	magbirô
journalist	peryodista
journey	biyahe/ paglakbáy
judge	huwés/hukom
juice	katás/dyus
to jump	tumalón
jumper (sweater)	switer
justice	katarungan

K

key	susì
kick	sipà
kick off	pagbunsód
to kill	patayín
kilogram	kilo
kilometre	kilometro
kind	mabaít (adj)
king	harì
kiss	halík
to kiss	halikán
Kiss me.	
Halikán mo akó. (inf)	
kitchen	kusinà
kitten	kutíng
knee	tuhod
knife	kutsilyo
to know(someone)	kilalá/kakilala
I know her.	
Kilalá ko hô siyá. (pol)	
Kakilala ko siyá. (inf)	
to know (something)	malaman
I don't know.	
Hindí ko alám.	

L

lace	puntás
lake	dagát-dagatan
land	lupà
languages	mgá wikà
large	malakí
last	hulí (adj)
last month	noóng isáng buwán
last night	kagabí
last week	noóng isáng linggó
last year	noóng isáng taón
late	hulí/náhulí
laugh	tawa/halakhák
law	batás
lawyer	abogado
laxatives	purgá/panunaw
laziness	katámaran
lazy	tamád
leaded (petrol/gas)	super
leader	pinunò
to learn	matuto
leather	balát
leathergoods	mgá bagay na yari sa balát
ledge	ungós
to be left (behind/over)	naiwanan/ nátirá
left (not right)	kaliwâ
left luggage	naiwanang bagahe
left-wing	makakaliwáng partido
leg	bintî
leg (in race)	bahagì
legalisation	legalisasiyón
legislation	pagbabatás
lens	lente
Lent	Kuwarisma
lesbian	binalaki/ lesbiyana/ tibô (col)

less	mas/kauntî
letter	sulat/liham
liar	sinungaling
library	aklatan
lice	kuto
to lie	magsinungaling
life	buhay
lift (elevator)	elebeytor
light (n)	liwanag/ilaw
sunlight	liwanag/sinag ng araw
moonlight	liwanag/sinag ng buwán
city lights	mgá ilaw ng siyudád
light (clear)	maliwanag
light bulb	bombilya/ilaw
lighter	pansindí
to like	gústo/gustó
line	guhit
lips	mgá labì
lipstick	lipistik
to listen	makiníg
little (small)	maliít
a little (amount)	kauntî
a little bit	katitíng
to live (life)	mabuhay
to live (somewhere)	tumirá
Long live ...!	
Mabuhay ... !	
local	lokál
local/city bus	bus
location	kinároroonán/ lugár
lock	kandado
to lock	susian

long	mahabà
long distance	pang-malayuan
long-distance bus	pang-malayuang bus
to look	tumingín
to look after (care for)	alagaan
to look for	hanapin
loose change	baryá
to lose	mawalâ
loser	talunan
loss	pagkawalá
a lot	marami
loud	maingay
to love	ibigin/ mahalín
lover	mangingibig
low	mababà
loyal	tapát
luck	kapalaran
lucky	masuwerte
luggage	bagahe/dalá- dalahan
luggage lockers	laker ng bagahe
lump	bukol
lunch	tanghalian
lunchtime	oras ng pananghalian
luxury	luho

M

machine	mákina
mad	galit na galit
made (of)	yarì sa

magazine	magasin	[It doesn't] matter.	
magician	salamangkero	Hindî bale.	
mail	koreo	[What's the] matter?	
mailbox	busón/hulugán	Anóng problema?	
	ng sulat	mattress	kutsón
main road	pangunahing	mayor	alkalde
	kalye	mechanic	mekánikó
main square	pangunahing	medal	medalya
	plasa	medicine	medisina
majority	ang	meditation	pagmumuni-
	nakarárami		muni
to make	gumawâ	to meet	makipagkita
make-up	pampagandá	member	kasapi
man	mamà	menstruation	regla
manager	mánedyer/	message	bilin
	tagapamahalà	metal	metál
manual worker	piyón	meteor	bulalakaw/
many	marami		taeng-bituín
Many happy returns!			(col)
Maligayang Batì sa iyóng		metre	metro
kaarawán! (inf)		midnight	hating-gabí
map	mapa	military service	panghukbong
Can you show me on the map?			paglilingkód
Puwede mong ipakita sa		milk	gatas
akin sa mapa? (inf)		millimetre	milimetro
marijuana	mariwana	million	milyón
market	palengke	mind	isip
marriage	kasál	a minute	isáng sandalî/
to marry	magpakasál		minuto
marvellous	kahanga-	Just a minute.	
	hangà	Sandalî lang. (inf)	
mass (Catholic)	misa	in [five] minutes	pagkalipas ng
massage	masahe		[limang]
mat	baníg		sandalî/
match	labanán		minuto
matches	pósporó	mirror	salamín

ENGLISH – PILIPINO

miscarriage	pagkaagas
to miss (feel absence)	hanáp-hanapin
mistake	kamalian
to mix	haluin
monastery	monasteryo
money	kuwarta/pera
monk	monghe
month	buwán
this month	ngayóng buwán
monument	monumento
moon	buwán
more	higít
morning (6am – noon)	umaga
mosque	moske
mother	iná/nanay
mother-in-law	biyenáng babae
motorboat	bangkang de-motór
motorcycle	motorsiklo
mountain	bundók
mountain hut	kubo sa bundók
mountain path	daán sa bundók
mountain range	kabundukan
mountaineering	pag-aakyát ng bundók
mouse	dagâ
mouth	bibíg
movie	sine/pelikulá
mud	putik

Mum	Inay/Mommy (English) Mamá (Spanish)
muscle	kalamanan
museum	museo
music	músika
musician	mánunugtóg
Muslim	Moslém
mute	pipe

N

name	pangalan
nappy	lampín
national park	pambansáng parke
nationality	nasyonalidád/ kabansaán
nature	kalikasan
nausea	pagduduwál
near	malapit
nearby hotel	kalapít na otél
necessary	kailangan
necklace	kuwintás
to need	kailanganin
needle (sewing)	karayom
needle (syringe)	hiringgilya
neither	sínumán ay hindî (someone) anumán ay hindî (something)
net	lambát
never	hinding-hindî; hindî kailanmán

new	bago	not yet	hindî pa
news	balità	novel (book)	nobela
newspaper	páhayagán	November	Nobyembre
newspaper in ...	páhayagán sa wikang ...	now	ngayón
		nun	madre
newspapers	mgá páhayagán	nurse	nars
New Year's Day	araw ng Bagong Taón		
		O	
New Year's Eve	bisperás ng Bagong Taón	obvious	halatâ
		ocean	karagatan
next	súsunód	offence	sala
next month	sa súsunód na buwán	office	tanggapan
		office work	gawain sa opisina
next to	katabí		
next week	sa súsunód na linggó	office worker	nagtatrabaho sa opisina
		often	malimit/ madalás
next year	sa súsunód na taón		
nice	magandá	oil (cooking)	langís-panglutò
nickname	palayaw	oil (crude)	langís na krudo
night	gabí	old	lumà
nine	siyám	old city	lumang lunsód
nineteen	labínsiyám	olive oil	langís ng oliba
ninety	siyámnapû	olives	mgá oliba
ninth	ikasiyám	on	sa
noise	ingay	on time	sa tamang panahon;
noisy	maingay		sa oras (col)
non-direct	hindî tulóy-tulóy		
		once; one time	minsan
none	walâ	one	isá
noon	tanghalì	one million	isang milyón
north	hilagà	only	lamang/ lang (col)
nose	ilóng		
notebook	kuwaderno	open	bukás
nothing	walâ	to open	pagbubukás

opera	óperá
operation	operasyón
opinion	palagáy
opposite	kabaligtarán (n)
or	ó
orange (colour)	kulay-dalandán
orchestra	orkestra
to order	umorder
ordinary	karaniwan
organise	magbuô
original	hindi kopya
other	ibá
outgoing	mapagkapwâ/ sosyál (col)
outside	nasa/sa labás
over	nasa/sa itaás
overcoat	oberkot
overdose	labis na dosis
to owe	may utang

I owe him.

May utang akó sa kanyá.

owner	may-arì

P

pacifier (dummy)	tsupón
package	pakete
packet (cigarettes)	pakete
padlock	kandado
page	páhiná
a pain	sakít
painful	masakít
painkillers	pampatáy-kirót
to paint	magpintá
painter	pintór
painting (the art)	pagpipintá

paintings	mgá larawan
pair (a couple)	mag-asawa
palace	palasyo
pan	kawalì
paper	papél
paraplegic	lumpó
parcel	pakete
parents	mgá magulang
a park	parke
to park	pumarada
parliament	batasan
part	bahagì
party	salu-salo
pass	lágusan
passenger	pasahero
passive	mahinahon
past	ang nakalipas (n)
path	daán/dáanan
patient	matiyagá (adj)
to pay	magbayad
payment	bayad
peace	kapayapaan
peak	tuktók
pedestrian	táong naglalakad
pen (ballpoint)	bolpen
pencil	lapis
penis	arì ng lalaki
penknife	lanseta
pensioner	pensiyonado
people	mgá tao
pepper	pamintá
percent	bahagdán
performance	palabás
permanent	pálagian

P

permission	pahintulot
permit	lisensiya
person	tao
personality	pagkatao
to perspire	pawisan
petition	pitisyón
petrol (gasoline)	gasolina
pharmacy	botika
photo	litrato

Can (May) I take a photo?
Máaarì ba akóng kumuha ng litrato? (inf)

photographer	potógrapó-litratísta
photography	potograpiya
pick	piko
pickaxe	palakól
to pick up	sunduín
pie	pastél
piece	planeta
plant	taním
to plant	magtaním
plastic	plastik
plate	plato
plateau	talampás
platform	entablado
play (theatre)	dulâ
to play (a game)	maglarô
to play (music)	tumugtóg
player (sports)	manlalarô
playing cards	baraha
to play cards	maglarô ng baraha; magbaraha
plug (bath)	pamasak
plug (electricity)	plag

pocket	bulsá
poetry	pánulaan
point (tip)	dulo/tulis
point (games)	punto
to point	iturò
police	pulís
politics	pulítiká
political speech	talumpating pampulítiká
politicians	pulítikó
pollen	pulbín
polls	poók na botohán
pollution	págpaparumí/polusyón
pool (swimming)	pálanguyan
poor	mahirap
popular	kilalá/popular
port	dáúngan
possible	posible

It's (not) possible.
Hindî hô iyán posible. (pol)

postcard	poskard
postage	bayad sa koreo
poster	paskil
post office	tanggapan ng koreo
pot (ceramic)	pasóng serámikó
pot (dope)	mariwana
pottery	paggawâ ng mga palayók
poverty	kahirapan
power	kapangyarihan
prayer	panalangin
prayer book	aklát-dásalan

Q

to prefer	mas gustó
pregnant	buntís
to prepare	maghandâ
present (gift)	regalo
present (time)	ngayón/ kasalukuyan
presentation	pagtatanghál
president	pangulò/ presidente
pressure	tindí/presyón
pretty	magandá
prevent	hadlangán
price	halagá/presyo
pride	pagpapahalagá sa sarili
priest	parè
prime minister	punong ministro
prison	bílangguan
prisoner	bilanggô
private	pribado
private hospital	pribadong ospitál
privatisation	pagsasapribado
to produce	magtanghál
producer	prodyuser
profession	propesyón
profit	tubò/kita
profitability	pagkákapaki- pakinabang
program	palatuntunan
projector	proyektór
promise	pangakò
proposal	panukala/ mungkahì

to protect	ipagtanggól
protected forest	mgá kagubatang inilíligtás
protest	protesta/ pagtutol
to protest	pumurutesta/ tutulan
public toilet	pálikurang pampúblikó
to pull	hilahín
pump	pambomba
puncture	butas
to punish	parusahan
puppy	tutà
pure	puro
purple	kulay-ube
to push	itulak
to put	ilagáy

Q

qualifications	mgá katangian
quality	urì
quarrel	away
quarter	sangkapat
queen	reyna
question	tanóng
to question	magtanóng
question (topic)	suliranin
queue	pila
quick	mabilís/ matulin
quiet (adj)	tahimik

R

rabbit	kuneho
radiator	radyetor
railroad	riles
railway station	istasyón ng tren
rain	ulán
It's raining.	
Umúulán.	
rally	malakíng pagtitipon
rape	panggagahasà
rare	bihirà
a rash	singaw sa balát
rat	dagâ
rate of pay	singíl
raw	hiláw
razor	pang-ahit
razor blades	mgá bleyd na pang-ahit
to read	magbasá
ready	handâ
to realise	matantô
reason	dahilán
receipt	resibo
to receive	tumanggáp
recent	di pa natátagalán
recently	kamakailán
to recognise	makilala
to recommend	irekomendá
record	talaan
record shop	tindahan ng plaka
recording	pagsasaplaka
red	pulá

referee	ang nagrere-komendá
reference	rekomendasyón
reflection (mirror)	larawan
reflection (thinking)	pagmumú-nimuni
to refund	magsolì ng bayad
to refuse	tanggihán
regional	pampoók
registered mail	rehistradong sulat
to regret	manghinayang
relationship	relasyón
to relax	maglibáng
religion	relihiyón
religious	relihiyoso
to remember	maalaala
remote	malayò
rent	upa
to rent	umupa/ umalkilá
to repeat	ulitin
republic	republika
reservation	pagpapáreserba
to reserve	magreserba
resignation	pagbibitíw
respect	galang
rest (relaxation)	pahingá
rest (what's left)	tirá
to rest	magpahingá
restaurant	restaurán
retired	retirado
to return	bumalík
return ticket	bálikang tiket

review	magbalík-aral
rhythm	indayog
rich (wealthy)	mayaman
rich (food)	masustansiya
to ride (a horse)	mangabayo
right (correct)	tamà
right (not left)	kanan
to be right	maging tamà
You're right.	
Tamà ka. (inf)	
civil rights	mgá karapatáng pangmamamayán
right now	ngayón mismo
right-wing	makanang partido
ring (on finger)	singsíng
ring (of phone)	kulilíng
I'll give you a ring.	
Tatawagan kitá. (inf)	
ring (sound)	tunóg
rip-off	dayà
risk	panganib
river	ilog
road (main)	kalye
road map	mapa ng kalye
to rob	magnakaw
rock	malakíng batô
rock climbing	pag-aakyát sa batuhán
[wall of] rock	pader na batô
rolling	gumugulong
romance	romansa
room	kuwarto
room number	número ng kuwarto

rope	lubid
round	bilóg
rowing	pagsasagwán
rubbish	basura
rug	pombra
ruins	mgá labî
rules	mgá pátakarán
to run	tumakbó

S

sad	malungkót
safe (adj)	ligtás
safe (n)	kaha de yero
safe sex	ligtás na seks
saint	santo
salary	suweldo
[on] sale	naká-baratilyo
sales department	sangáy na may kinalaman sa pagtitinda
salt	asín
same	magkapareho
sand	buhangin
sanitary napkins	pasadór
Saturday	Sábadó
to save	mag-ipon
to say	sabihín
to scale/climb	umakyát
scarves	mgá bandana
school	páaralán
science	aghám
scientist	dalúb-aghám/ sayantist
scissors	guntíng

screen	puting-tabing	seven	pitó
script	iskrip	seventeen	labimpitó
sculpture	inukit na bagay	seventh	ikapitó
sea	dagat	seventy	pitumpû
seaside	tabíng-dagat	several	mgá ilan
seat	úpuan	to sew	tahiín
seatbelt	sinturóng pangseguro	sex	kasarián/seks
		sexy	seksi
second (n)	saglít	shade; shadow	lilim;anino
second	ikalawá	shampoo	panggugò/ syampu
secretary	sekretarya		
to see	mákita	shape	hugis

We'll see!

Mákikita natin!/Tignan natin!

I see. [understand]

Naiintindihán ko.

See you later.

Hanggáng mamayâ. (inf)

See you tomorrow.

Hanggáng bukas. (inf)

		to share (with)	bahaginan
		to shave	mag-ahit
		she	siyá
		sheep	tupa
		sheet (bed)	kumot
		sheet (of paper)	pilas
		shell	kabibi
		shelves	mgá sálansanan
		ship	bapór/barkó
self-employed	may-sariling trabaho	to ship	ipadalá ng bapór
selfish	maramot/ madamot	shirt	kamisa
self-service	kani-kanyáng kuha	shoe shop	tindahan ng sapatos
to sell	magtindá	shoes	mgá sapatos
to send	magpadalá	to shoot	barilín
sensible	makatwiran	shop	tindahan
sentence (words)	pangungusap	to go shopping	mamilí
sentence (prison)	sentensiya	short (length)	maiklî
to separate	maghiwaláy	short (height)	mababà
series	hanay	short films	mgá maiiklíng pelikula
serious	seryoso		
service (help)	serbisyo	short stories	mgá maiiklíng kuwento
service (religious)	kulto		

shortage	kulang	single woman	dalaga
shorts	korto	single (unique)	íisá
shoulders	balikat	single room	kuwartong pang-isahan
to shout	sumigáw		
a show	palabás	sister	kapatíd na babae
to show	ipakita		

Can you show me on the map?
Puwede hô ninyóng ipakita sa akin sa mapa? (pol)

shower	dutsa	to sit	umupô
shrine	dambanà	six	anim
to shut	isará	sixteen	labíng-anim
shy	mahiyain	sixth	ikaanim
sick	may-sakít	sixty	animnapû
a sickness	karamdaman	size	sukat
side	tabí	skiing	pag-iiski
a sign	senyas	to ski	mag-iski
to sign	pumirma/ pirmahán	skin	balát
		sky	langit
		to sleep	matulog
		sleeping pills	tabletas na pampatulog

Sign here.
Pumirma kayó dito. (pol)
Sign this.
Pirmahán ninyó itó. (pol)

signature	pirmá	sleepy	antók
silk	seda	slow/slowly	mabagal
of silver	na pilak	small	maliit
similar	katulad	a smell	amóy
simple	simple/payák	to smell	amuyín
sin	kasalanan	to smile	ngumitî
since (May)	buhat noóng (Mayo)	to smoke a cigarette	manigarilyo
to sing	umawit	to smoke a cigar	manabako
singer	mang-aawit	to smoke a pipe	magpipa
single (person)	walâ pang asawa	soap	sabón
		soap opera	dulâ
single man	binatà	soccer	saker
		social-democratic	sosyál-demokratiko
		social sciences	aralíng panlipunan

social welfare	kapakanáng panlipunan
socialist	sosyalista
solid	sólido
some	ilán
somebody	tao; may tao
something	anumán
sometimes	paminsan-minsan
son	anák na lalaki
song	awit
soon	mámayâ
I'm sorry.	
Dinaramdam ko.	
sound	tunóg
south	timog
souvenir	subenir
souvenir shop	tindahan ng subenir
space	alangaang
to speak	magsalitâ
special	di-pangkaraniwan
specialist	dalubhasà/ espesiyalista
speed	bilís/tulin
speed limit	takdáng bilís
spicy (hot)	maanghang
sport	larô/isport
sportsperson	manlalarò
a sprain	pilay
spring (season)	tagsiból
spring (coil)	muwelye
square (shape)	parísukát/ kuwadrado
square (in town)	plasa
stadium	istadyum

stage	tanghalan
stairway	hagdanan
stamps	selyo
standard (usual)	karaniwan
standard of living	pámantayan ng pamumuhay
stars	mgá bituín
to start	magsimulâ
station	istasyón
statue	istatwa
to stay (remain)	mamalagì
to stay (somewhere)	manirahan
to steal	magnakaw
steam	usok
steep	matarik
step	hakbáng
stomach	tiyán
stomachache	sakít ng tiyán
stone	bató
stoned (drugged)	duróg
stop	hintuan
to stop	humintô
Stop!	
Hintô!	
storm	bagyó
story	kuwento
stove	kalán
straight	tuwíd
strange	katakátaká
stranger	dayuhan
stream	batis
street	kalye
strength	lakás
a strike	welga
on strike	naka-welga

string	talí
stroll; walk	pasyál
strong	malakás
stubborn	matigás ang ulo
student	istudyante
studio	istudyo
stupid	tangá
style	istilo
suburb	panirahang lugár sa labás ng lunsód
suburbs of ...	sa labás ng lunsód ng ...
success	tagumpáy
to suffer	magdusà
sugar	asukal
suitcase	maleta
summer	tag-inít/tag-araw
sun	araw
sunglasses	sanglas
sunny	maaraw
sunrise	pagtaás ng araw
sunset	paglubóg ng araw
Sure.	Sigurado.
surname	apelyido
a surprise	sorpresa
to survive	makaligtás
sweet	matamís
sweetheart	kasintahan
to swim	lumangóy
swimming	paglangóy
swimming pool	pálanguyan

swimsuit	damit panlangoy
sword	espada
sympathetic	maawaín
synagogue	simbahan ng mga hudyó
syringe	hiringgilya

T

table	mesa
table tennis	pingpong
tail	buntót
to take (away)	alisín
to take (the train)	magtrén
to take photographs	kumuha ng litrato
to talk	magsalitá
tall	mataás
tampons	mgá tampon
tasty	masaráp/ malinamnám
tax	buwís
taxi stand	puwesto ng taksi
teacher	gurò/titser
teaching	pagtuturò
team	koponan
tear (crying)	luhà
technique	paraán/ pamamaraán
teeth	mga ngipin/ ipin (col)
telegram	telegrama
telephone	teléponó
to telephone	tumawag sa teléponó

telephone office	tanggapan ng teléponó
telescope	largabista
temperature	temperatura
temple	templo
ten	sampû
tennis	tenis
tennis court	láruan ng tenis
tent	tolda
tent pegs	pako ng tolda
tenth	ikasampú
terrible	terible/ nakatátakot
test	suriin
to thank	magpasalamat
Thank you.	Salamat
theatre	teatro
they	silá
thick	makapál
thief	magnanakaw
thin (material)	manipís
thin (person)	payát
to think	umisip
third	sangkatló
third (adj)	ikatló
thirsty	uháw
thirteen	labintatló
thirty	tatlumpû
thought	isip
thousand	sanlibo/isang libo
three	tatló
three of a kind	tatlóng magkaka-pareho

three-quarters	tatlong-kapat
throat	lalamunan
ticket	tiket
ticket collector	kolektór ng tiket
ticket office	takilya
tide	paglakí at pagliít ng tubig sa dagat
high tide	taog
low tide	kati
tight	masikíp
timetable	taláorasán
tin (can)	lata
tin opener	abre-lata/ pambukás ng lata
tip (gratuity)	pabuya
tired	pagód
tissue paper	tisyu
toad	palakà
toast (bread)	tustadong tinapay
tobacco	tabako
tobacco kiosk	kiyosko ng tabako
today	ngayóng araw
together (for two people)	magkasama
together (for more than two)	magkakasama
toilet paper	tisyu/papel sa kubeta
toilets	mga pálikuran/ mgá CR

English	Pilipino
tomorrow	bukas
tomorrow afternoon/ evening	bukas ng hapon/ gabí
tomorrow morning	bukas ng umaga
tonight	ngayóng gabí
too (as well)	din/rin
too expensive	masyadong mahal
too much/many	masyadong marami
tooth	ngipin
toothache	sakít ng ngipin
toothbrush	sipilyo ng ngipin
toothpaste	tutpeyst
torch (flashlight)	lente/plaslayt
to touch	hipuin
tour	paglalakbáy
tourist	turista
tourist informa- tion office	tanggapan ng turismo
towards	patungò sa
towel	tuwalya
tower	tore
town (large, city)	lunsód/siyudád
town (small)	bayan
toxic	may lason
track (car-racing)	kárerahán
track (footprints)	bakás
track (sports)	larô sa takbuhan
track (path)	daán
trade union	unyón ng mgá manggagawà

English	Pilipino
traffic	trápikó
traffic lights	mgá ilaw pantrápikó
trail/route	daán/ruta
train	tren
train station	istasyon ng tren
tram	trambiya
to translate	magsalin
to travel	maglakbáy
travel agency	ahensiyang panturismo
traveller	manlalakbay
travel (books)	mga aklát tungkol sa paglakbay
tree	punò
trek	paglalakád
trendy (person)	mahilig sa uso
trip	biyahe
trousers	pantalón
truck	trak
trust	tiwalà
to trust	magtiwalà
truth	katotohanan
It's true.	Totoó iyán.
to try	subukan
to try (attempt)	magtangkâ
T-shirt	kamiseta
tune	tono
Turn left.	Likô sa kaliwâ.
Turn right.	Likô sa kanan.
TV	TV

V

twelve	labindalawá
twenty	dalawampû
twice	dalawáng beses
twin beds	dalawáng magkalapit na kama
twins	kambál
two	dalawá
two pairs	dalawáng pares
two tickets	dalawáng tiket
to type	magmakinilya
typical	típikó
tyres	mga gulóng

U

umbrella	payong
underpants	salawál na panloób
to understand	máintindihán
unemployed	waláng trabaho
unemployment	kawalaán ng trabaho
unions	mgá unyón
universe	sanlibután
university	pámantasan
unleaded	regulár
unsafe	mapanganib/ peligroso
until	hanggáng
unusual	hindî karaniwan
up	pataás
uphill	paakyát

urgent	ápurahan
useful	kapaki- pakinabang

V

vacant	bakante
vacation	bakasyón
vaccination	bakuna
valley	lambák
valuable	mahalagá
value (price)	halagá
vegetable	gulay
vegetarian	na waláng karné
vegetation	pagtubò
vein	ugát
venereal disease	sakit sa babae
venue	lugár
very	lubhâ

('Very' can also be expressed by attaching the prefix napaká to the adjective or adverb, see Grammar chapter, under Adjectives heading.)

view	tánawin
village	baryo
vine	baging
vineyard	tániman ng ubas
virus	mikrobyo
visa	bisa
to visit	dumalaw
vitamins	mgá bitamina
voice	tinig/boses
volume	dami
to vote	bumoto

W

Wait!	
Hintáy! (inf)	
waiter	weyter
waiting room	silíd-hintayan
to walk	lumakad
wall (inside)	dingdíng
wall (outside)	padér
want	gústo/gustó
war	digmaan
wardrobe	aparadór
warm	mainit
to warn	balaan
to wash (something)	hugasán
to wash (oneself)	maghugas
washing machine	makináng panlabá
watch	reló
to watch (a movie)	manoód
to watch (look after)	bantayán
water	tubig
water bottle	bote ng tubig
waterfall	talón
wave	alon
way	daán

Please tell me the way to ...
Puwede hô ba ninyóng sabihin sa akin ang daán patungong ...? (pol)
Which way?
Alíng daán?

Way Out	Lábásan

we	tayo (the English 'we')
	kamí (excludes the person spoken to)
weak	mahinà
wealthy	mayaman
to wear	magsuót/ gumamít (col)
weather	panahón
wedding	kasál
wedding present	regalo para sa kasál
week	linggó
this week	ngayóng linggó
weekend	Sábado at Linggó
to weigh	timbangín
weight	bigát/timbáng
welcome	pagsalubong
welfare	kapakanán
well	mabuti
west	kanluran
wet	basâ
what	anó

What is he saying?
Anóng sinasabi niyá? (inf)
What time is it?
Anóng oras na? (inf)
What are you doing?
Anóng ginágawâ mo? (inf)
[What's the] matter?
Anóng problema?

wheel	gulóng
wheelchair	silyang de gulóng

when · kailán/kelan
  When's the next flight to (Cebu)?
  Kelan hô ang súsunód na
  flight papuntáng (Cebú)?
where · nasaán/saán
  Where is the bank?
  Násaán hô ang bangko? (pol)
white · putî
who · sino
  Who is it?
  Sino iyán? (inf)
  Who are they?
  Sino ba silá? (inf)
whole · buô
why · bakit
  Why is the museum closed?
  Bakit hô sarado ang museo?
  (pol)
wide · malapad
wife · maybahay
wild animal · mabangís na
  hayop
to win · manalo
wind · hangin
window · bintanà
windscreen · pananggáng-
  hangin
wine · alak
wings · mgá pakpák
winner · panalo
winter · taglamig
wire · kawad/alambre
wise · matalino
with · ng/sa pamama-
  (by means of) · gitan ng

within · sa loób
within an hour · sa loób ng
  isáng oras
without · walâ
without filter · waláng filter
woman · babae/ale
wonderful · nápakagaling
wood · kahoy
wool · lana
word · salitâ
work · gawain/trabahó/
  hanap-buhay
to work · magtrabaho
work permit · pahintulot
  magtrabaho
workshop · talyér
world · mundó/daigdig
worms` · mgá bulate
worried · balisá
wound · sugat
to write · sumulat
writer · mánunulat
wrong · malî
  I'm wrong. (my fault)
  Kasalanan ko.
  I'm wrong. (not right)
  Malî akô.

Y

year · taón
this year · ngayóng taón
yellow · diláw
yesterday · kahapon
yet · pa

you	kayó (pol)
	ikáw (inf)
	kayó (pol,pl)
	kayó (inf, pl)
young	batà
youth (collective)	kabataan

Z

zebra	sebra
zero	sero
zodiac	sodyako

The Pilipino alphabet (Abakada) has fewer letters than the English alphabet. The order is the same except for the letter 'k' which comes after 'b' and 'ng' which is a separate letter and comes after 'n'.

English entries in the list which may have no single-word counterparts in Pilipino have been paraphrased. English words more commonly used than their Pilipino counterparts have been given in English in some of the phrases.

A

abalá	busy
abaniko	fan (hand-held)
abenida	avenue
abogado	lawyer
abre-lata	tin opener
Abríl	April
aklát	book
aklát památnubay	guidebook
aklatan	library
aklát-dásalan	prayer book
akó	I
aksidente	accident
aktibista	activist
adwana	customs
agahan	breakfast
aghám	science
aginaldo	gift
ahedres	chess
ahensiyang panturismo	travel agency
alagaan	to look after (care for)
alahas	jewellery
alak	wine
alambre	wire
alangaang	atmosphere
albularyo	herbalist
ale	woman
alerdyi sa pulbín	hayfever
alérhiya/ álerdyi	allergy
Alís dyán!	
Get lost!	
alisín	to take (away)
alkalde	mayor
almusál	breakfast
alon	wave
altár	altar
amá	father
amerikana	coat
amo (col)	employer
amóy	a smell
amuyín	to smell
anák na babae	daughter

A

anák na lalaki — son
anarkista — anarchist
anemya — anaemia
anim — six
animnapû — sixty
anino — shadow
anó — what
  Anóng oras na? (inf)
  What time is it?
  Anóng ginágawâ mo? (inf)
  What are you doing?
  Anóng problema?
  What's the matter?
  Anóng sinasabi niyá? (inf)
  What's he saying?
antena — antenna
antók — sleepy
anumán — something
ang Bibiliyá — the Bible
  Ang galing!
  Great!
ang nagrerekomendá — referee
ang nakalipas — past
  [kalahating oras] na ang nakalipas
  [half an hour] ago
ang nakarárami — majority
ang paglinis — cleaning (n)
aparadór — wardrobe
apat — four
apatnapû — forty
apelyido — surname
apendiks — appendix

aplaya — beach
apó — grandchild
apóy — fire (controlled)
apurado — in a hurry
ápurahan — urgent
araling panlipunan — social sciences
araw ng Bagong Taón — New Year's Day
araw ng pagsilang — date of birth
araw ng Pasko — Christmas Day
araw — day
araw — sun
araw-araw — daily
arì ng lalaki — penis
arina — flour
arkitekto — architect
arkitektura — architecture
arma — weapon
artista — artist
asawa — husband
ásidó — acid (drug)
asín — salt
aso — dog
aspirina — aspirin
asukal — sugar
asúl — blue
at — and
atletik — athletics
away — quarrel
awit — song
awto — car
  Ayós!
  Agreed!

B

babae	woman
babaeng kaibigan	girlfriend
baka	cow
bakante	vacant
bakás	track (footprints)
bakasyón	holidays
bakasyón	vacation
bakeshop	cake shop
bakit	why

Bakit hô sarado ang museo? (pol)
Why is the museum closed?

baklâ	gay
bakod	fence
bakuna	vaccination
badíng (col)	gay
bagahe	luggage
baging	vine
bago	new
baguhan	amateur
bagyo	storm
bahagdán	percent
bahagì	leg (in race)
bahagì	part
bahagian	to share (with)
bahay	house
balaan	to warn
balabal	cloak
balabal	coat
balát	leather
balát	skin
balkón/ balkonahe	balcony

baldé	bucket
baléy	ballet
balikat	shoulders
balisá	worried
balità	news
balíw	crazy
banda	band (music)
bandila	flag
baníg	mat
bantayán	to watch (look after)
bantóg	famous
banyaga	foreign
banyo	bathroom
bangkang de-motór	motorboat
bangketa	footpath
bangko	bank
bangkâ	a small native boat
bapór/barkó	ship
baraha	playing cards
barilín	to shoot
barò	dress
baryá	loose change
baryá	change (coins)
baryo	village
basâ	wet
baság	broken (glass)
baság-ulero	aggressive
basbasán	to bless
basket	basket
basketbol	basketball
basura	garbage
basura	rubbish
batà	baby/child

B

batà	young
batang babae	girl
batang lalaki	boy
batás	law
batasan	parliament
batiryá	battery
batis	stream
bató	stone
bawat	each
bayad	payment
bayad sa koreo	postage
bayan	town (small)
baybáy	coast
benda	bandage
bendisyunán	to bless
bentiladór	fan (machine)
berde	green
bestido	dress
beysbol	baseball
bibíg	mouth
bigát	weight
bigyán	to give
Máaarì mo ba akóng bigyán ...? (inf)	
Could you give me ...?	
bihirà	rare
bilang libangan	for fun
bilang ng pasport	passport number
bilanggô	prisoner
bílangguan	prison
bilangguan	jail
bilangin	to count
bilibid	jail
bilin	message
bilís	speed

bilóg	round
bilyár	billiards
binabaé	gay
binalaki	lesbian
binatà	single man
bingí	deaf
bintanà	window
bintî	leg
binyág	baptism
birò	joke
biruin	to make fun of
bisa	visa
bisikleta	bicycle
bisikleta	bike
bisperás ng Bagong Taón	New Year's Eve
bisperás ng Paskó	Christmas Eve
biyahe	trip
biyahe	journey
biyenáng babae	mother-in-law
biyenáng lalaki	father-in-law
Biyernes	Friday
biyograpiya	biography
blangket	blanket
boksing	boxing
bola	ball
bolpen	pen (ballpoint)
bombilya	light bulb
boses	voice
botas	boots
botas na panglakad nang malayuan	
hiking boots	
bote/botelya	bottle
bote ng tubig	water bottle

K

botika	pharmacy/chemist
braso	arm
bukas	tomorrow
bukas ng hapon	tomorrow afternoon
bukas ng umaga	tomorrow morning
bukás	open
bukid	farm
bukol	lump
bukong-bukong	ankle
bugháw	blue
buhangin	sand
buhat noóng	since (May)
buhay	life
buhók	hair
bulág	blind
bulaklák	flower
búlalakaw	meteor
bulsá	pocket
bulwagan	foyer
bumalík	to return
bumilí	to buy

Gústo kong bumilí... (inf)
I'd like to buy ...
Saán akó puwedeng bumilí ng tiket? (inf)
Where can I buy a ticket?

bumoto	to vote
bundók	mountain
buntalà	comet
buntís	pregnant
buntót	tail
buô	whole
buriko	donkey

buról	hill
bus	local;city bus
bus na pamprobinsiya	bus (intercity)
busón	mailbox
butas	puncture
butó	bone
buwán	month
buwán	moon
Buwenas!	Good luck!
buwís sa kita	income tax
buwís	tax

K

kaakit-akit	charming
kaarawán	birthday
kabaligtarán	opposite
kabansaán	nationality
kabataan	youth (collective)
kabayo	horse
kabibi	shell
kabukiran	countryside
kabuhayan	economy
kabundukan	mountain range
kabutihan	advantage
kakilala	to know (someone)

Kakilala ko siyá. (inf)
I know her.

kagabí	last night
kagamitán na pangsisid	diving equipment
kagát	bite (dog, insect)

K

kaha de yero	safe (n)	kamakalawá	day before yesterday
kaha	cash register		
kahanga-hangà	marvellous	kamalian	mistake
kahapon	yesterday	kamatayan	death
kahero (m)/ kahera (f)	cashier	kamáy	hand
		kambál	twins
kahirapan	poverty	kambíng	goat
kahit anó	any	kambyo	gear stick
kahon ng unang panglunas	first aid kit	kámerá	camera
		kamí	we (excludes the person spoken to)
kahón	box		
kahoy	wood		
kahoy na panggatong	firewood	kamisa	shirt
		kamiseta	T-shirt
kaibigan	friend	kanan	right (not left)
kailán	when		
Kailán hô ang súsunód na flight papuntáng (Cebú)? When's the next flight to (Cebú)?		Likô sa kanan. Turn right.	
		kanina	a while ago
kailangan	necessary	kandado	lock
kailanganin	to need	kandado	padlock
kalahatì (n)	half	kandilà	candle
kalahating litro	half a litre	kani-kanyáng kuha	self-service
kalamnan	muscle		
kalán	stove	kanluran	west
kalapít na otél	nearby hotel	kanselahín	to cancel
kalendaryo	calendar	kanto	corner
kalesa	gig	kapakanán	welfare
kalikasan	nature	kapakanáng panlipunan	social welfare
kaliwâ	left (not right)		
		kapakí- pakinabang	useful
Likô sa kaliwâ. Turn left.			
		kapalaran	luck
kalusugan	health	kapaligirán	environment
kalye	road (main)	kapangyarihan	power
kama	bed	kapatíd na babae	sister
kamakailán	recently		

kapatid na lalaki	brother
kapayapaan	peace
kapinsalaán	disability
kapwà	both
karagatan	ocean
karamdaman	a sickness
karaniwan	ordinary
karaniwan	standard (usual)
karapatáng pantao	human rights
karayom	needle (sewing)
kárerahán	track (car-racing)
karetela	gig
kargahín	to carry
kartón	carton
kartún	cartoons
kasál	marriage
kasál	wedding
kasalanan	fault (someone's); sin

Kasalanan ko.
I'm wrong. [my fault]

kasalukuyan	present (time)
kasama	companion
kasama	included
kasamahán	colleague
kasapî	member
kasarián	sex
kasí	because
kasiguruháng panlipinan	social security
kasintahan na babae	girlfriend
kasintahan	sweetheart
kastilyo	castle

katabí	next to
katakatakâ	strange
katámaran	laziness
katarungan	justice
katás	juice
katawán	body
katedrál	cathedral
kathâ	fiction
katí	itch
kati	low tide
katoliko (m)/ katolika (f)	Catholic
katotohanan	truth
katulad	similar
kauntì	less
kauntî	a little (amount); few
kawad	wire
kawalâ (hindî nakatali)	free (not bound)
kawalaán ng trabaho	unemployment
kawali	pan
kawili-wili	interesting
kalye	street
kayó	you (inf, pl)/ you (pol, pl)
kayumanggî	brown
kelan	when
keso	cheese
kilalá	popular
kilalá	to know (someone)

Kilalá ko hô siyá. (pol)
I know her.

kilo	kilogram

kilometro	kilometre
kinároroonán	location
kinsena	fortnight
kiyosko ng tabako	tobacco kiosk
klats	clutch (car)
kliyente	client
kolehiyo	college
kolektór ng tiket	ticket collector
komedya	comedy
komersyante	business person
kometa	comet
komiks	comics
komportable	comfortable
kompromiso	engagement
komunista	communist
komunyón	communion
konserbatibo	conservative
konsiyerto	a concert
konsulado	consulate
kontrata	contract
koponan	team
koreo	mail
koreong ekspres	express mail
koreong panghimpapawíd	air mail
korte	court (legal)
korto	shorts
kotse	car
kristál	glass
kristiyano	Christian
krus	cross (religious)
kubo sa bundók	mountain hut

kulang	insufficient
kulay	colour
kulay dalandan	orange (colour)
kulay-abó	grey
kulay-kapé	brown
kulay-ube	purple
kuliglíg	cricket (insect)
kulilíng	ring (of phone)

Tatawagan kitá. (inf)
I'll give you a ring.

kulto	service (religious)
kumain	to eat
kumbento	convent
kumita	to earn
kumot	sheet (bed)
kumpanyá	company
kumpas	compass
kumpisál	confession (religious)
kumuha ng litrato	to take photographs

Kumustá.
Hello.
Helo!
Hello! (answering telephone)

kung	if
kupón	coupon
kursó	diarrhoea
kuryente	electricity
kusinà	kitchen
kutíng	kitten
kuto	lice
kutsilyo	knife
kutsón	mattress
kuwaderno	notebook

kuwadrado	square (shape)
Kuwarisma	Lent
kuwarta	money
kuwartáng papél	banknotes
kuwarto	room
kuwartong pang-isahan	single room
kuwartong-tulugán	bedroom
kuwenta	bill
kuwento	story
kuwintás	necklace

D

daán/dáanan	path
daán sa bundók	mountain path
daán	track (path)
daán	way

Alíng daán?
Which way?
Puwede hô ba ninyóng sabihin sa akin ang daán patungong ...? (pol)
Please tell me the way to ...

daán	trail; route
dagâ	rat; mouse
dagat	sea
dagát-dagatan	lake
dahil	because
dahilán	reason
daigdíg	Earth/world
dais	dice; die
dalá-dalahan	baggage
dalaga	single woman
dalawá	two
dalawampû	twenty
dalawáng beses	twice
dalawáng magkalapit na kama	twin beds
dalawáng tiket	two tickets
dalhín	to bring
dalirì	finger
dalisdís	cliff
dalúb-aghám	scientist
dalubhasà	specialist
dama	draughts
damahán	chess board
dambanà	shrine
damdamin	feelings
dami	volume
damít	clothing
damit-pampaligò	bathing suit
damit panlangoy	swimsuit
damó	grass (also slang for marijuana)
dati	before
dáungan	harbour; port
dayà	rip-off
dayuhan	stranger
demokrasya	democracy
demonstrasyón	demonstration
dentista	dentist
depekto	fault (in manufacture)

E

detalye	detail
di pa natátagalán	recent
dibdíb	breast/chest
dibuho	design
diksiyunariyo	dictionary
digmaan	war
diláw	yellow
di-maunawaan	incomprehensible
din	also; too (as well)
Dinaramdam ko.	I'm sorry.
dingdíng	wall (inside)
di-pagkakápantáy-pantáy	inequality
di-pangkaraniwan	special
di-propesyunál	amateur
direktór	director
disbentaha	disadvantage
disenyong inukit sa metál	etching
Disyembre	December
disyerto	desert
dito	here
diyabétikó	diabetic
Diyós	God
doble	double
doktór	doctor
dokumentaryo	documentary
drama	drama
dugô	blood
dulâ	play (theatre); soap opera
dulo	point (tip)
dumalaw	to visit
dumating	to come; arrive
duróg	stoned (drugged)
dutsa	shower
duyan	hammock
dyim	gym
dyimnastik	gymnastics
dyip	jeep

E

ekonomiya	economy
ekspres	express
edád	age
edukasyón	education
elebeytor	elevator
elebeytor	lift (elevator)
elektrisidád	electricity
embahada	embassy
embahadór (m)/ embahadora (f)	ambassador
empleado (m)/ empleada (f)	employee
entablado	platform
Epipanya	Epiphany
eroplano	aeroplane
erowina	heroin
espada	sword
espesiyalista	specialist

G

gabí	evening
gabí	night
galang	respect
galeriya	art gallery

galing sa	descendent
galit	anger
galít na galít	mad
galit	cross (angry)
gamót	drug
gansâ	goose
garapón	jar
gasolina	petrol
gatas	milk
gawain sa bahay	housework
gawain sa konstruksiyón	construction work
gawain sa opisina	office work
gawain	work
gawín	to do

Anóng ginágawâ mo? (inf)
What are you doing?
Hindî ko hô iyón ginawâ.(pol)
I didn't do it.

gitara	guitar
giya	guide (person)
gobyerno	government
gol	goal
gramo	gram
grupong anti-nuclear	antti-nuclear group
gubat	forest
guhit	line
gulang	age
gulay	vegetable
gulóng	wheel
gumamít (col)	to wear
gumawâ	to make
gumugulong	rolling

gurò	teacher
gusalì	building
gústo	to like; to want

Gústo kong bumilí... (inf)
I'd like to buy ...
Gústo naming pumuntá sa ... (inf)
We'd like to go to ...

gutóm	hungry
gutom	hunger
guwapo	handsome
guwarnasyón	harness

H

habang-buhay	forever
hadlangán	prevent
hagdanan	stairway
hakbáng	step
halakhák	laugh
halagá ng pálitan	exchange rate
halagá	value (price)/ worth
halálan	elections
halík	kiss
halikán	to kiss

Halikán mo akó. (inf)
Kiss me.

| halimbawà | example |

Halimbawá, ...
For example, ...
Halina.
Let's go.

| halos | almost |
| haluin | to mix |

H

hamón	ham
hanap-buhay	work
hanáp-hanapin	to miss (feel absence)
hanapin	to look for
hanay	series
hanbag	handbag
handâ	ready
hangganan	border
Hanggáng bukas. (inf)	
See you tomorrow.	
Hanggáng mamayâ. (inf)	
See you later.	
hanggáng (Mayo)	until (May)
hangin	wind
hangin	air
hapunan	dinner
harì	king
hating-gabí	midnight
Helo!	
Hello! (answering telephone)	
híkain	asthmatic
higít	more
hilagà	north
hilahín	to pull
hiláw	raw
hiló	dizzy
hímatayin	epileptic
himnasyo	gym
himpilan	channel (TV)
hináharáp	future
hindi kopya	original
hindî	no/not
Hindî akó sang-ayon.	
I don't agree.	

Hindî bale.	
[It doesn't] matter.	
Hindî hô iyán possible. (pol)	
It's (not) possible.	
Hindî iyón importante. (inf)	
It's not important.	
Hindî ko alám.	
I don't know.	
Hindî ko hô iyón ginawâ. (pol)	
I didn't do it.	
Hindî ko alám.	
I don't know.	
Hindî ko hô magagawâ iyán. (pol)	
I can't do it.	
hindî isinama	excluded
hindî kailanmán	never
hindî karaniwan	unusual
hindî nakatali	free (not bound)
hindî pa	not yet
hindî tulóy-tulóy	non-direct
hinding-hindî	never
hinete	jockey
hintuan	stop
Hintáy! (inf)	
Wait!	
Hintô!	
Stop!	
hintuan ng bus	bus stop
hipuin	to touch
hiringgilya	needle; syringe
homoseksuwál	homosexual
hukom	judge
húkúman	court (legal)

hugasán	to wash (something)
hugis	shape
hulaan	to guess
hulí (adj)	last
hulílate	
hulugán ng sulat	mailbox
humangà	to admire
humingá	to breathe
humingî	to ask (for something)
humintô	to stop
humirám	to borrow
hustó	enough
huwés	judge

I

ibá	different
ibá	other
ibigin	to love
ibon	bird
ikaanim	sixth
ikaápat	fourth
ikalawá	second
ikalimá	fifth
ikapitó	seventh
ikasampú	tenth
ikasiyám	ninth
ikatló	third (adj)
ikáw	you (sg)
ikawaló	eighth
ID (English)	identification card
idrowing	to draw

idyota	idiot
iguhit	to draw
íisá	single (unique)
ilagáy	to put
ilán	some
ilaw	light (n)
ilaw	light bulb
ilaw pantrápikó	traffic lights
ilog	river
ilóng	nose
imigrasyón	immigration
impatso	indigestion
impeksiyón	infection
importante	important

Importante iyón. (inf)
It's important.
Hindi iyón importante. (inf)
It's not important.

iná	mother
inaasikaso	looking after (entertaining)
inahíng manók	hen
Inay	Mum
indayog	rhythm
industriya	industry
inhinyeriya	engineering
inhinyero	engineer
iniksiyón	injection
iniksiyunán	to inject
init	heat
intindihin	to care (about)
inukit na bagay	sculpture
ínumin	a drink

Ingat lang!
Careful!

ingay	noise

L

Inglatera	England
Inglés	English
ipakita	to show

Puwede hô ninyóng ipakita sa akin sa mapa?
Can you show me on the map?

ipadalá ng bapór	to ship
ipágdiwang	to celebrate (an event)
ipagtanggól	to protect
ipin (col)	teeth
irekomendá	to recommend
isá	one
isáng dosena	a dozen
isáng kamang pandalawahan	a double bed
isáng kuwartong pandalawahan	a double room
isang libo	thousand
isang milyón	one million
isáng sandalí	a minute

Sandalí lang. (inf)
Just a minute.

isará	to shut
iskrip	script

Iskyus lang hô. (pol)/
Iskyus lang. (inf)
Excuse/Pardon me.

isdâ	fish
isip	mind
isip	thought
isla	island
isport	sport
istadyum	stadium
istasyón	channel (TV); station
istasyón ng bus	bus station
istasyón ng tren	railway station
istatwa	statue
istilo	style
istudyo	studio
istudyante	student
itanghál	to exhibit
itáy	dad
itím	black
itiniraryo	itinerary
itulak	to push
iturò	to point

L

laban sa	against
laban	fight
labanán	match
lábasan	exit

Lábasan
Way Out

labimpitó	seventeen
labindalawá	twelve
labinlimá	fifteen
labinsiyám	nineteen
labintatló	thirteen
labíng-isá	eleven
labíng-anim	sixteen
labíng-apat	fourteen
labíng-waló	eighteen
labis na dosis	overdose
lakás	strength
laker ng bagahe	luggage lockers
lagì	always/forever
lagnát	fever

lágusan	pass
lahát	all
lalamunan	throat
lalawigan	country
lamang	only
lambák	valley
lambát	net
lampín	nappy
lana	wool
lanseta	penknife
lang (col)	only
langaw	fly
langgám	ant
langís na krudo	oil (crude)
langis ng oliba	olive oil
langís-panglutò	oil (cooking)
langit	sky
lapis	pencil
larawan	reflection (mirror)
largabista	binoculars
largabista	telescope
larô sa takbuhan	track (sports)
larô	game; sport
láruan	court (sports)
láruan ng tenis	tennis court
lasíng	to be drunk
lata	can (tin/aluminium)
legalisasiyón	legalisation

lente	lens
lente	torch (flashlight)
lesbiyana (col)	lesbian
libíng	funeral
libingan (n)	grave
libre	free (of charge)
libró	book
Likô sa kaliwâ.	Turn left.
Likô sa kanan.	Turn right.
likód	back (body)
ligtás na seks	safe sex
ligtás	safe (adj)
liham	letter
lilim	shade
limá	five
limampú	fifty
lindól	earthquake
Linggó ng Pagkabuhay	Easter
linggó	week
lipistik	lipstick
lisensiya	driver's licence
lisensiya	permit
litrato	photo
Máaarì ba akóng kumuha ng litrato? (inf) Can (May) I take a photo?	
liwanag	light (n)
liwanag ng araw	sunlight
liwanag ng buwán	moonlight
lokál	local

M

lokó-lokó (m)/ loká-loká (f) — crazy

lola/ lolo — grandmother/ grandfather

LSD — acid (drug)

lubhâ — very

('Very' can also be expressed by attaching the prefix napaká to the adjective or adverb, see Grammar chapter, under Adjectives heading.)

lubid — rope

lugár — space/venue

luhà — tear (crying)

luho — luxury .

lumà — old

lumaban — fight against

lumabás kasama — to go out with

lumakad — to walk

lumang lunsód — old city

lumangóy — to swim

lumpó — paraplegic

lunsód — city; large town

lupà — earth (soil); land

M

máaarì — able (to be); can

Máaarì ba akóng kumuha ng litrato? (inf)
Can (May) I take a photo?

Máaarì mo ba akóng bigyán ...? (inf)
Could you give me ...?

Magágawâ namin itó. (inf)
We can do it.

Puwede mo bang ipakita sa akin sa mapa? (inf)
Can you show me on the map?

maaga — early

Maaga pa.
It's early.

maalaala — to remember

maanghang — spicy (hot)

maaraw — sunny

maawain — sympathetic

maayá (adj) — pleasant

mababà — low

mababà — short (height)

mabagal — slow; slowly

mabaít (adj) — kind

mabangís na hayop — wild animal

mabigát — heavy

mabilís — quick/fast

mabuhay — to live (life)

Mabuhay ... !
Long live ...!

Mabuhay!
Good health!; Cheers!

mabuti — well

mabuting otél na mabuti — good hotel

makakaliwáng partido — left-wing

makákita — to find

makaligtás — to survive

makalimutan — to forget

Nakakalimutan ko. (inf)
I forget.

Kalimutan mo na iyón!;
Huwag mong intindihin
iyón! (inf)
Forget about it!; Don't worry!

makakanang — right-wing
partido

makapál — thick

makapuntos — to score

makaramdám ng ...
to feel ...

makatwiran — sensible

makilala — to recognise

mákiná — engine;
machine

makináng — washing
panlabá — machine

makiníg — to listen

makipágkita — to meet

makipágtípanan — to date

makita — to see

Hanggáng bukas. (inf)
See you tomorrow.
Hanggáng mámayâ. (inf)
See you later.
Mákikita/Tignan natin!
We'll see!
Naiintindihán ko.
I see. [understand]

madalás — often

madalí — easy

madalíng-araw — dawn

madamot — selfish

madayà — crafty

madilím — dark

madre — nun

madulâ — dramatic

madumí — dirty

mag-ahit — to shave

mag-anak — family

magandá — beautiful

magandá — nice

magandá — pretty

Magandáng gabí.
Good evening/night.
Magandáng hapon.
Good afternoon.
Magandáng umaga.
Good morning.

mag-asawa — pair (a couple)

mágasín — magazine

mag-away — to fight

magbalík — return

magbaraha — to play (cards)

magbasá — to read

magbayad — to pay

magbirô — to joke

magbisikleta — to cycle

magbuô — to organise

magkahalagá — to cost

Magkano ang papuntá sa ...?
How much does it cost to go
to ...?
Mahál na mahál.
It costs a lot.

magkáilâ — to deny

magkakasama — together (more
than two)

magkampo — to camp

Máarì ba kamíng magkampo
dito? (pol)
Can we camp here?

magkapareho — same

M

magkaroón;	to have (see
may	page 33.)
Mayroón ba kayong ...? (pol)	
Do you have ...?	
Mayroón hô akong ... (pol)	
I have ...	
magkasama	together (for two people)
magdugô	to bleed
magdusa	to suffer
maghandâ	to prepare
maghiwaláy	to separate
maghugas	to wash (oneself)
magináw	cold (adj)
maging tamà	to be right
Tama ka. (inf)	
You're right.	
maginhawà	comfortable
mag-ipon	to save
mag-isá	alone
mag-iski	to ski
maglakád nang malayò	to hike
maglakbáy	to travel
maglagáy	to bribe
maglaró	to play (a game)
maglarô ng baraha	to play cards
maglibáng	to enjoy (oneself)
maglibáng	to have fun
maglibáng	to relax
maglutò	to cook
magmakinilya	to type
magmaneho	to drive
magnakaw	to rob

magnakaw	to steal
magnanakaw	thief
magpabagsák	to bribe (col)
magpadalá	to send
magpaguniguní	to hallucinate
magpahingá	to rest
magpakasál	to marry
magpalít	to change
magpalít	to exchange (money)
magpasalamat	to thank
magpasiyá	to decide
magpatayô	to build
magpintá	to paint
magpipa	to smoke a pipe
magreserba	to book (make a booking)
magreserba	to reserve
magsalin	to translate
magsalitâ	to speak
magsalitâ	to talk
magsasaka	farmer
magsayáw	to dance
magsimulâ	to start
magsinungaling	to lie
magsoli ng bayad	to refund
magsuhol	to bribe
magsuót	to wear
magtalo	to argue
magtangkâ	to try [attempt]
magtanghál	to produce
magtaním	to plant
magtanóng	to ask (a question)
magtindá	to deal/sell
magtiwalà	to trust

PILIPINO – ENGLISH

Magumpisá na tayo!
Bon appétit!

mag-window-shopping	to [go] window-shopping
magyelo	to freeze
mahabà	long
mahál	expensive

Mahál na mahál.
It costs a lot.

Mahál na Araw	Holy Week
mahalagá	valuable; important
mahalín	to love; to care (for someone)
mahilig sa uso	trendy (person)
mahinà	weak
mahinahon	passive
mahirap	difficult/poor
mahiyain	shy
maiklî	short (length)
mainit	hot/warm

Mainit.
It's hot.
Mainit ngayóng araw.
It's hot today.
Mainit ang kapé.
The coffee is hot.

mainit na tubig	hot water
máintindihán	to understand
maingay	loud
maingay	noisy
malakas	strong
malakí	big
malakí	great
malakí	large

malakíng batò	rock
malakíng pagtitipon	rally
malalim	deep
málaman	to know (something)

Hindî ko alám.
I don't know.

malamíg	cold (adj)

Ang lamíg.
It's cold.

malamíg na tubig	cold water
malapad	wide
malapit	near
malayò	far
malayò	remote
maleta	suitcase

Malî akô.
I'm wrong.
Maligayang batì sa iyóng káarawán! (inf)
Happy birthday!
Maligayang Bati!
Many happy returns!; Congratulations!
Maligayang paglakbay!
Bon voyage!

maliít	little (small)
maliít na bundók	hill
malimit	often
malinamnám	tasty
malinis na otél	clean hotel
malinis	clean
malî	wrong

211

Kasalanan ko.
I'm wrong. (my fault)
Malî akô.
I'm wrong. (not right)

maliwanag	light (clear)
malungkót	sad
mamà	man
Mamá	Mum
mamalagì	to stay (remain)
mámayâ	soon
mamilí	to go shopping
manabako	to smoke a cigar
managinip	to dream
manalo	to win
mandaraya	a cheat

Mandaraya!
Cheat!

mánedyer	manager
mang-aawit	singer
mangangalakal	business person
manggagawà sa pábriká	factory worker
manghál ng baraha	deck (of cards)
manibela	handlebars
manigarilyo	to smoke a cigarette
manipís	thin (material)
manirahan	to stay (some-where)
manlalakbáy	traveller
manlalarò	player (sports)
manlalarò	sportsperson
manók	chicken
manoód	to watch (a film)
mánunugtóg	musician

mánunulá	writer
manghinayang	to regret
manghuhulà	fortune teller
mangingibig	lover
maóng	jeans
mapa	map
mapa ng kalye	road map

Puwede mong ipakita sa akin sa mapa? (inf)
Can you show me on the map?

mapagkapwâ	outgoing
mapágmahál	caring
mápahiyâ	embarassed
mapanganib	unsafe
marami	a lot
marami	many
maramot	selfish
mariwana	marijuana
mariníg	to hear
mariwana	hash
martilyo	hammer
marumí	dirty
mas gustó	to prefer
mas	less
masahe	massage
masakít	painful
masamâ	bad
masaráp	tasty
masayá	happy
masikíp	tight
masirà	to break
maskí anó	any
masustansiya	rich (food)
masuwerte	lucky
masyadong mahál	too expensive

212

masyadong marami	too much; many	may-depekto	faulty
matá	eye	mayroón	to have
mataás	high/tall	may sakit	sick
mataás na páaralán	high school	may sariling trabaho	self-employed
matabá	fat	may sirà	faulty
matalino	brilliant/wise	may utang	to owe
matamís	sweet	May utang ako sa kanya.	
matantô	to realise	I owe him.	
matapang	brave	medalya	medal
matarik	steep	medisina	medicine
matigás ang ulo	stubborn	mekánikó	mechanic
matigás	hard	mesa	table
matindí	intense	metál	metal
matiyagá (adj)	patient	metro	metre
mátuklasán	to discover	mga aklát tungkol sa paglakbay	travel (books)
matulin	quick/fast		
matulog	to sleep	mgá antibyotiko	antibiotics
matuto	to learn	mgá antigo	antiques
matuyô	to dry (clothes)	mgá antolohiya	anthologies
maulap	cloudy	mgá bandana	scarves
Maulop.		mgâ batà	children
It's foggy.		mga bawal na gamót	dope (drugs)
mawalâ	to lose		
may erkon	air-conditioned	mgá bilang	figures
may kapansanan	disabled	mgá bitamina	vitamins
may lason	toxic	mgá bleyd na pang-ahit	razor blades
may sipón	to have a cold		
mayaman	rich (wealthy)	mga botante	electorate
may-arì	owner	mga butones	buttons
maybahay	wife	mga kagamitán	equipment
Mayroon ba kayong ...? (pol)		mgá kagubatang inilíligtás	protected forest
Do you have ...?			
Mayroón hô akong ... (pol)		mgá kampeonato	championships
I have ...		mga kard	cards

M

mgá katangian	qualifications
mgá kondom	condoms
mga kuweba	caves
mgá CR	toilets
mga daán para sa paglakad nang malayò	hiking routes
mga damong panggamót	herbs
mgá eladong pagkain	frozen foods
mga gulóng	tyres
mgá hardín	gardens
mgá hayop	animals
mgá ilan	several
mgá ilaw ng siyudád	city lights
mgá ipis	cockroaches
mgá labì	lips
mga labî	ruins
mga larawan	paintings
mgá magulang	parents
mgá maiikling kuwento	short stories
mgá maiikling pelikula	short films
mga malalaking tindahan	department stores
mga manikà	dolls
mga ngipin	teeth
mgá oliba	olives
mgá pagdating	arrivals
mgá páhayagán	newspapers
mgá pakpák	wings
mga pálikuran	toilets
mga panindáng yarì sa balát	leathergoods
mga pátakarán	rules
mgá pelikula ng panahong itó	contemporary films
mga produktong yarì sa gatas	dairy products
mgá sálansanan	shelves
mgá sapatos	shoes
mgá sigarilyo	cigarettes
mgá tagahangà	fans (of a team)
mga tamból	drums
mga tampon	tampons
mgá táo	people
mgá tenga	ears
mgá ubas	grapes
mgá unyón	unions
mgá wikà	languages
mgá bulati	worms
mgá hikaw	earrings
mgá papél ng sigarilyo	cigarette papers
mikrobyo	virus
milimetro	millimetre
milyón	million
minsan	once; one time
minuto	a minute
misa	mass (Catholic)
Mommy	Mum
monasteryo	monastery
monghe	monk
monumento	monument
moske	mosque
Moslém	Muslim
motorsiklo	motorcycle

PILIPINO – ENGLISH

N

mukhá	face
mulî	again
multá	a fine
mundó	Earth/world
mungkahì	proposal
murang otél	cheap hotel
museo	museum
músika	music
muwelye	spring (coil)

N

na	already
na gintô	of gold
na pilak	of silver
na waláng karné	vegetarian
naká-baratilyo	[on] sale
nakákaalíw/ nakákalibáng	entertaining
nakakaantók/ nakakainíp	boring
nakakainís/ nakákaasár	pain in the neck
nakakakilabot/ nakakatakot	horrible
Nakakalimutan ko. (inf) I forget.	
nakakatakot	awful
nakasakáy	aboard
nakauslíng matarik na bató	crag
naka-welga	on strike
nagtatrabaho sa opisina	office worker
nagtitinda ng bawal na gamót	drug dealer

Nagyeyelo. It's frosty.	
nahíhibáng	delirious
náhulí	late
naiiníp	bored
Naiintindihán ko. I see. [understand]	
naiwanan	to be left behind
naiwanang bagahe	left luggage
nanay	mother
nápakagalíng	excellent
nápakagalíng	wonderful
nars	nurse
nasa gulang	adult
nasa ibáng bansa	abroad
nasa	below; over; outside; at the back (behind); behind; inside; between; beside
násaán	where
Násaán hô ang bangko? (pol) Where is the bank?	
nátirá	to be left over
nasyonalidád	nationality
negatibo	film (negatives)
negosyante	businessman/ woman
negosyo	business

215

nerbyos bago magka-regla	pre-menstrual tension
nobela	novel (book)
Nobyembre	November
nobyo	boyfriend
nobyo/nobya	fiancé/fiancée
noón	before
noóng isáng buwán	last month
noóng isáng linggó	last week
noóng isáng taón	last year
número ng kuwarto	room number

NG

ng unang panahón	ancient
ng	with (by means of)
ng/sa panahóng itó	contemporary (adj)
ngambá	misgiving; doubt; fear
ngayón mismo	right now
ngayón	now; present (time)
ngayóng araw	today
ngayóng buwán	this month
ngayóng gabí	tonight
ngayong hapon	this afternoon
ngayóng linggó	this week
ngayóng taón	this year
ngipin sa likód	tooth (back)
ngumitî	to smile

O

ó	or
oberkot	overcoat
opera	opera
operasyon	operation
oras (ng pag-alís)	time (departure time)
oras ng pananghalian	lunchtime
orkestra	orchestra
oso	bear
ospitál	hospital
otél na mura	cheap hotel

P

pa	yet
paá	foot
paakyát	uphill
Paalam.	Goodbye.
paano	how
Paano ko hô mararatíng ang ...? (pol)	How do I get to ...?
Paano sabihin ...? (inf)	How do you say ...?
páaralán	school
pábriká	factory
pabuyá	tip (gratuity)
pakete	package; packet (cigarettes)
pako ng tolda	tent pegs
pader na bato	[wall of] rock

padér	wall (outside)
pág papasok	admission
pag-aakyát ng bundók	mountaineering
pag-aakyát sa batuhán	rock climbing
pag-alís	departure
págawaan	factory
pagbabantáy ng batà	childminding
pagbabatás	legislation
pagbibisikleta	cycling
pagbibitíw	resignation
pagbunsód	kick off
pagkaagas	miscarriage
pagkaatraso	delay
pagkagumon sa bawal na gamót	drug addiction
pagkain ng batà	baby food
pagkákapaki-pakinabang	profitability
pagkakápantáy-pantáy	equality
pagkakátaón	chance
pagkalagalág	homelessness
pagkalipas ng (anim) na araw	in (six) days
pagkalipas ng (limang) sandalî	in (five) minutes
pagkamáma-mayán	citizenship
pagkápahiyâ	embarassment
pagkatao	personality
pagkatapos	after
pagkawalá	loss

pagduduwál	nausea
paggawâ ng mga palayók	pottery
paghahardín	gardening
pagieskrima	fencing
pag-iiski	skiing
paglakád na may giya	guided trek
paglakad nang malayò	hiking
paglakí at pagliit ng tubig sa dagat	tide
paglalakád	trek
paglalakbáy	tour; journey
paglangoy	swimming
paglipád ng eruplano	flight
paglubog ng araw	sunset
pagmumuni-munì	meditation
pagmumúnimuni	reflection (thinking)
pagód	tired
pagpapaalís	dismissal
pagpapahalagá sa sarili	pride
pagpapalaglág	abortion
pagpapáreserba	reservation
págpaparumí	pollution
Pagpaumanhín hô ninyó. (pol) to apologise for a mistake or a wrong done	
pagpigil ng pagbubuntís	contraception

pagpipintá	painting (the art)
pagsalubong	welcome
pagsambá	worship
pagsasagwán	rowing
pagsasaka	agriculture
pagsasamantalá	exploitation
pagsásanay	workout
pagsasaplaka	recording
pagsasapribado	privatisation
pagsayáw	dancing (n)
pagsisid	diving (n)
pagsisirà ng kagubatan	deforestation
pagsusurì sa dugô	blood test
pagtaas ng araw	sunrise
pagtatanghál	presentation
pagtatangì	discrimination
pagtayô	erection
pagtubò	vegetation
pagtutol	protest
pagtuturò	teaching
pagyarì sa kamáy	handicrafts
páhayagán	newspaper
pahintulot para makapagtrabaho	work permit
páhiná	page
pahingá	intermission; rest (relaxation)
pahintulot	permission
palabás	a show; performance
palakâ	toad
pálakasan	athletic

palakol	pick/pickaxe
palakól na pangyelo	ice axe
palagáy	opinion
pálagian	permanent
pálagiang koleksiyón	permanent collection
palanguyan	swimming pool
palapag	floor (storey)
palasyo	palace
palátandaan	identification
palatuntunan	program
palayaw	nickname
palengke	market
pálikurang pampúblikó	public toilet
paliligô	bath
páliguan	bathroom
páliparan	airport
pálitan	exchange
paltós	blister
pámahalaán	government
pamamaraán	technique
pámantasan	university
pámantayan ng pamumuhay	standard of living
pamasak	plug (bath)
pamaypáy	fan (hand-held)
pambansáng parke	national park
pambomba	pump
pambukás ng bote	bottle opener
pambukás ng lata	can opener
pamilya	family

pamimitás ng prutas	fruit picking
paminggalan	cupboard
paminsan-minsan	sometimes
pamintá	pepper
pampagandá	make-up
pampahid sa balat laban sinag ng araw	sunblock
pampainit	heater
pampatáy-kirót	painkillers
pampigil ng pagbubuntis	contraceptives
pampoók	regional
panaderyá	bakery
panahón	epoch/weather
panahón ng panunungkulan	term of office
panalangin	prayer
panalo	winner
pananggáng-hangin	windscreen
panayám	interview
pandaigdíg	international
pandarayuhan	immigration
pandisimpekta	antiseptic
panirahang lugár sa labas ng lunsod	suburb
panlahát	general
pansindí	lighter
pantalón	trousers
Pantástikó! Fantastic!	
panukala	proposal

pánulaan	poetry
pang-ahit	razor
pangakò	promise
pangalan	name
pangalang kristiyano	christian name
pang-alís ng amóy	deodorant
pangangabayo	horse riding
panganib	risk
panggagahasà	rape
pangguguló	harrassment
panghukbong paglilingkod	military service
pang-malayuan	long distance
pang-malayuang bus	long-distance bus
pangulò	president
pangunahing kalye	main road
pangunahing plasa	main square
pangungusap	sentence (words)
panunaw	laxatives
papá	dad
papasukin	to admit
papél	paper
papél sa kubeta	toilet paper
papeles ng awto	car owner's title
paraán	technique
parang	field
parke	a park
parè	priest
pareho	both
parísukát	square (shape)

parmasya	chemist	pero	but
paróroonán	destination	peryodista	journalist
paruparó	butterfly	petsa	date (time)
parusahan	to punish	piko	pick/pickaxe
pasâ	a bruise	pila	queue
pasadór	sanitary napkins	pilas	sheet (of paper)
pasahero	passenger	pilay	a sprain
paskíl	poster	pilm	film (camera)
pasò	a burn	pinakamagalíng	best
pasóng serámikó	pot (ceramic)	pinsalà	injury
		pintô	door
pasport	passport	pintór	painter
pastél	pie	pinunò	leader
pasyál	stroll; walk	pingpong	table tennis
pataás	up	pipe	mute
patag	flat (land)	pirmá	signature
patalastás	job advertisement	pirmahán	to sign
patawarin	to forgive	Pirmahán ninyó itó. (pol)	
patáy	dead	Sign this.	
patayín	to kill	pistá	festival
patnugot	editor	Pistá ng Tatlóng Harì	
patungô sa	towards	Epiphany	
Paumanhín hô. (pol)		pitisyón	petition
to ask permission to leave		pitó	seven
pawisan	to perspire	pitumpû	seventy
payák	simple	piyér	harbour
payaso	clown	piyesta	festival
payát	thin (person)	piyesta	holiday
payò	advice	piyón	manual worker
payong	umbrella	plag	plug (electricity)
Pebrero	February	planeta	planet
pelíkulá	film (cinema); film camera	plasa	square (in town)
		plaslayt	torch (flashlight)
peligroso	dangerous	plastik	plastic
pensiyonado	pensioner	plato	plate
pera	money	polusyón	pollution

pombra	rug
poók na botohán	polls
posible	possible
Hindî hô iyán posible. (pol)	
It's (not) possible.	
poskard	postcard
pósporó	matches
potograpiya	photography
potograpó litratísta	photographer
presidente	president
presyo	price
presyón	pressure
presyón ng dugô	blood pressure
pribado	private
pribadong ospitál	private hospital
probinsiya	country
prodyuser	producer
propesyón	profession
protesta	protest
proyektór	projector
pulá	red
pulbín	pollen
pulbós ng batà	baby powder
pulgás	flea
pulís	police
pulítiká	politics
pulítikó	politicians
pulót-gatâ	honeymoon
pulót-pukyutan	honey
pulubi	beggar
pumarada	to park
pumarito	to come
pumasok	to enter

pumayag	to allow
pumilì	to choose
pumirmá	to sign
Pumirma kayó dito. (pol)	
Sign here.	
Pirmahan ninyó itó. (pol)	
Sign this.	
pumuntá	to go
Halina.	
Let's go.	
Gústo naming pumuntá sa ... (inf)	
We'd like to go to ...	
Tulóy-tulóy lang hô. (pol)	
Go straight ahead.	
pumurutesta	to protest
punô	full
punò	tree
puntás	lace
punto	point (games)
puntód	grave
punuín	to fill
purgá	laxatives
puro	pure
pusà	cat
pusò	heart
pustá	a bet
putbol	football
putî	white
putik	mud
puting-tabing	screen
putulin	to cut
puwede	able (to be); can
puwesto ng taksi	taxi stand
puwít	bum/ass

R

radyetor	radiator
regalo para sa kasál	wedding present
regalo	present (gift)
regalo	gift
regla	menstruation
regulár	unleaded
rehistradong sulat	registered mail
rehistro ng awto	car registration
rekomendasyón	reference
relasyón	relationship
relihiyón	religion
relihiyoso	religious
reló na may-panggising	alarm clock
reló	clock
reló	watch
republika	republic
resibo	receipt
restaurán	restaurant
retirado	retired
reyna	queen
riles	railroad
rin	also; too (as well)
romansa	romance
round trip tiket	return (ticket)
ruta	trail; route

S

sa	on
saán	where
sa babâ	below
sa kabilâ	across
sa haráp ng	in front of
sa itaás	over
sa labás	outside
sa likód	at the back (behind)
sa loób	within; inside
sa loób ng isáng oras	within an hour
sa mgá	among
sa pagitan	between
[sa] rotonda	[at the] round about
sa súsunód na buwán	next month
sa súsunód na linggó	next week
sa súsunód na taón	next year
sa tabí	beside
sa tamang panahón; sa oras (col)	on time
Sábadó	Saturday
Sábado at Linggó	weekend
sabihin	to say
sabón	soap
saker	soccer
sakít	a pain/disease
sakít ng ngipin	toothache
sakít ng tiyán	stomachache
sakít ng ulo	a headache
sakít sa babae	venereal disease
Saklolo!	Help!

sakunâ	accident	seguro	insurance
saglít	second (n)	sekretarya	secretary
sagót	answer	seks	sex
sahíg	floor	seksi	sexy
sala	offence	seloso (m)/	jealous
salamangkero	magician	selosa (f)	
Salamat.		selyo	stamps
Thank you.		Semana Santa	Holy Week
salamín	mirror	senténsiyá	sentence
salamín	glass		(prison)
salawál na	underpants	sentimetro	centimetre
panloób		sentro ng	city centre
salitâ	word	siyudád	
salu-salo	party	senyas	a sign
samakalawá	day after	serbisyo	service
	tomorrow	sero	zero
sampán	champagne	sertipíko	certificate
sampû	ten	seryoso	serious
sandaán	a hundred	siklista	cyclists
Sandalí lang. (inf)		Sigurado.	
Just a minute.		Sure.	
sanlibo	thousand	silá	they
sanlibután	universe	silangan	east
santo	saint	silíd-hintayan	waiting room
sangáy	branch	silya	chair
sangkapat	quarter	silyang de	wheelchair
sangkatló	third	gulóng	
sanggól	baby/infant	simbahan	church
sanglas	sunglasses	simhahan ng	synagogue
sapát	enough	mga hudyó	
sarado	closed	simple	simple
sarhán	to close	sinag ng araw	sunlight
sayá	fun	sinag ng buwán	moonlight
sayantist	scientist	sine	movie
sebra	zebra	sinehán	cinema
seda	silk	sining	art

sining na klásikó	classical art	sosyál-demokratiko	social-democratic
sinisero	ashtray	sosyalista	socialist
sino	who	subenir	souvenir
Sino ba silá? (inf)		subukan	to try
Who are they?		sukat	size
Sino iyán? (inf)		sukláy	comb
Who is it?		suklî	change (coins)
sinsilyo	coins	sugapà	addiction
sinturóng pangseguro	seatbelt	sugapà sa erowina	heroin addict
sinungaling	liar	sugat	wound
singáw sa balat	a rash	sulat	letter
singíl	rate of pay	suliranin	question (topic)
singsíng	ring (on finger)	sumakáy	to board (ship)
sipà	kick	sumakáy sa kabayo	to ride (a horse)
sipilyo ng ngipin	toothbrush	sumáng-ayon	to agree
sipilyong pambuhók	hairbrush	Hindî ako sang-ayon.	
		I don't agree.	
sipón	a cold	Ayós!	
sirâ	broken (out of order)	Agreed!	
		sumigáw	to shout
sirain	to destroy	sumulat	to write
sirko	circus	sumunód	to follow
siyá	he/she	sunduín	to pick up
siyám	nine	sunog ng araw sa balat	sunburn
siyámnapû	ninety		
siyudád	city; large town	sunog	fire (uncontrolled)
sobre	envelope		
sodyako	zodiac	super	leaded (petrol; gas)
sólido	solid		
sorbetes	icecream	suriin	test
sorpresa	a surprise	surot	bedbug
sosyál (col)	outgoing	susì	key
		susian	to lock

PILIPINO – ENGLISH

T

Susmaryosep!
(An expression used by the older
generation which is hardly used
now. It is actually the contracted
form of Hesus, Maria, Hosep or
Jesus, Mary and Joseph.)

suso	breasts
súsunód	next
suweldo	salary
sward (col)	gay
switer	jumper (sweater)
syampu	shampoo

T

taás	altitude
tabako	tobacco
tabí	side
tabíng-dagat	seaside
tabíng-dagat	beach
tabletas na pampatulog	sleeping pills
takdáng bilís	speed limit
takilya	ticket office
takot	fear
takót sa	to be afraid of
taeng-bituín (col)	meteor
tagapagturò	instructor
tagapamahagì	distributor
tagapamahalà	curator
tagapamahalà	director
tag-aráw	summer
tagasanay	coach (trainer)
tagá-yuropa	european
tag-inít	summer
taglagás	autumn (fall)

taglamíg	winter
tagsibol	spring (season)
tagumpay	success
tahiín	to sew
tahimik	quiet (adj)
talaan	record
tálaan ng mga puntos	scoreboard
taláarawán	diary
talambuhay	biography
talampás	plateau
taláorasán	timetable
talì	string
talón	waterfall
talumpating pampulitiká	political speech
talunan	loser
talyér	garage (car repair shop); workshop
tamà	right (correct)
Tamà ka. (inf) You're right. Tama na! Enough!	
tamád	lazy
tánawin	view
taním	plant
tániman ng ubas	vineyard
tanké ng gas	gas cartridge
tanóng	question
tangá	stupid
tanggapan	office
tanggapan ng koreo	post office

225

tanggapan ng teléponó	telephone office
tanggapan ng turismo	tourist information office
tanggapín	to accept
tanggihán	to refuse
tanghalan	exhibition
tanghalan	stage
tanghalì	noon
tanghalian	lunch
tao	person; somebody; husband (col)
taog	high tide
taong naglalakad	pedestrian
taón	year
tapát	loyal
tapón	cork
tapusin	to end
tárangkahan	gate
tasa	cup
Tatawagan kitá. (inf) I'll give you a ring.	
tatay	father
tatló	three
tatlóng magkakapareho	three of a kind
tatlong-kapat	three-quarters
táunan	annual
tawa	laugh
tawad	discount
tayâ	a bet
tayo	we (includes the person being spoken to)
tayog	altitude
teatro	theatre
teatrong klásikó	classical theatre
telebisiyón	television
telegrama	telegram
teléponó	telephone
temperatura	temperature
templo	temple
tenga	ear
tenis	tennis
terible	terrible
tibí	constipation
tibô (col)	lesbian
tiket	ticket
timbâ	bucket
timbáng	weight
timbangín	to weigh
timog	south
tindahan	shop
tindahan ng kámerá	camera shop
tindahan ng damít	clothing store
tindahan ng gulay	greengrocer
tindahan ng isdâ	fish shop
tindahan ng libró	bookshop
tindahan ng plaka	record shop
tindahan ng sapatos	shoe shop
tindahan ng subenir	souvenir shop

tindí	pressure	tsokolate	chocolate
tingnán	to check	tsupón	dummy/ pacifier
tinig	voice		
tiníp	silent	tubig	water
tinitibí	to be constipated	tubò	profit
tinto	red wine	tuhod	knee
tinig	voice	tukâ	beak
tinggâ	lead (metal)	tuktók	peak
típanan	date (appoint- ment)	tuláy	bridge
		tulin	speed
típikó	typical	tulong	aid (help)
tirá	rest (what's left)	Tulóy-tulóy lang hô. (pol) Go straight ahead.	
tírahan	address	túluyan	accommodation
tisyu	tissue paper; toilet paper	tumakbó	to run
		tumalón	to jump
títuló	degree	tumanggáp	to receive
tiwalà	trust	tumawag sa teléponó	to telephone
tiwalí	corrupt		
tiya	aunt	tumingín	to look
tiyák	sure/certain	tumirá	to live (some where)
tiyakín	to confirm (a booking)		
		tumugtóg	to play (music)
tiyán	stomach	tumulong	to help
tolda	tent	tunóg	ring/sound
tono	tune	tupa	sheep
tore	tower	turista	tourist
Totoó iyán. It's true.		tustadong tinapay	toast (bread)
trabaho	job	tutà	puppy
trak	truck	tutpeyst	toothpaste
trambiya	tram	tutulan	to protest
trápikó	traffic	tuwalya	towel
tren	train	tuwíd	straight
tsapa	badge	tuwiran	direct
tses	chess	TV	TV

U

ubó	a cough
ugát	vein
uháw	thirsty
ulán	rain
Umúulán.	
It's raining.	
ulap	cloud
ulî	again
ulitin	to repeat
ulo	head
umakyát	to scale/climb
umaga	morning (6am - 12 noon)
umalkilá	to hire/rent
Saán ako puwedeng umalkila ng bisikleta? (inf)	
Where can I hire a bicycle?	
umalís	to depart (leave)
umangkás	to hitchhike
umawit	to sing
umiiskor (col)	to chat up
uminóm	to drink
umisip	to think
umorder	to order
umupa	to hire/rent
umupô	to sit
una	first
náuuná	ahead
ungós	ledge
unyón ng mgá manggagawà	trade union
upa	rent

úpuan	seat
urì	quality
urì ng dugô	blood group
usá	deer
usok	steam

W

wakás	end
walâ pang asawa	single (person)
walâ	none/nothing/ without
waláng bayad	free (of charge)
waláng filter	without filter
waláng kulay	B&W (film)
waláng trabaho	unemployed
waláng-lamán	empty
waláng pasok	holiday
waló	eight
walumpû	eighty
watawat	flag
welga	a strike
weyter	waiter

Y

yakap	a cuddle
yagyág	canter
yarì sa	made (of)
yarí sa kamáy	handmade
yarì sa tansô	(made) of brass
yayà	babysitter
yelo	ice

CROSSWORD ANSWERS

Accommodation

Across

2. bisa	visa
3. pinakámurang	cheapest
8. dutsa	shower
9. bareta	bar
(ng sabón)	(of soap)

Down

1. bintanà	window
2. bimpo	face cloth
3. punda	pillow case
4. kampingan	camping ground
5. adrés	address
6. gabí	night
7. kumot	sheet

Around Town

Across

2. sigaret	cigarette
(bendor)	vendor
4. palengke	market
6. maglalakô	ambulant peddlar
8. bawal	prohibited
9. palasyo	palace

Down

1. aklatan	library
2. sinsilyo	coins
3. tulay	bridge
5. embahada	embassy
7. plasa	town square

Shopping

Across

1. may (filter)	filtered
4. syampo	shampoo
7. pilm	film
	[for a camera]
8. mantekilya	butter
9. kuwintás	necklace

Down

1. modista	dressmaker
2. yosì	cigarettes
3. tutpeyst	toothpaste
5. lampin	nappy
6. hikaw	earrings

In the Country

Across

2. lárgabista	binoculars
5. kuliglíg	cricket [insect]
7. pako	tent pegs
(para sa tolda)	
8. tág-ulan	rainy season
10. kalán	stove
11. aso	dog

Down

1. elepante	elephant
3. bulaklák	flower
4. talón	waterfall
6. gubat	forest
9. giya	guide

Health

Across

1.	tibí	constipation
5.	kuto	lice
6.	nahihilo	dizzy
8.	impatso	indigestion
9.	paá	foot
10.	bulak	cotton balls

Down

2.	bato	kidney
3.	trangkaso	influenza
4.	ipin	teeth
5.	kalamanan	muscle
7.	bukol	lump

Time, Dates & Festivals

Across

2.	kagabí	last night
5.	ngayón	now
7.	Maligayang (Paskó)	Merry Christmas
9.	Abríl	April
10.	Mahal na Araw [3 words]	Holy Week

Down

1.	(ngayón) taón	this year
3.	(sa) isáng bukas [2 words]	day after tomorrow
4.	Nobyembre	November
6.	kanina	a while ago
8.	gabí	night

INDEX

LONELY PLANET PHRASEBOOKS

Complete your travel experience with a Lonely Planet phrasebook. Developed for the independent traveller, the phrasebooks enable you to communicate confidently in any practical situation – and get to know the local people and their culture.

Skipping lengthy details on where to get your drycleaning ironed, information in the phrasebooks covers bargaining, customs and protocol, how to address people and introduce yourself, explanations of local ways of telling the time, dealing with bureaucracy and bargaining, plus plenty of ways to share your interests and learn from locals.

Arabic (Egyptian)
Arabic (Moroccan)
Australian
  *Introduction to Australian English,
  Aboriginal and Torres Strait languages*
Baltic States
  *Covers Estonian, Latvian and
  Lithuanian*
Bengali
Brazilian
Burmese
Cantonese
Central Asia
Central Europe
  *Covers Czech, French, German,
  Hungarian, Italian and Slovak*
Eastern Europe
  *Covers Bulgarian, Czech, Hungarian,
  Polish, Romanian and Slovak.*
Ethiopian (Amharic)
Fijian
French
German
Greek
Hindi/Urdu
Indonesian
Italian
Japanese
Korean
Lao
Malay
Mandarin
Mediterranean Europe
  *Covers Albanian, Croatian, Greek,
  Italian, Macedonian, Maltese, Serbian
  and Slovene*

Mongolian
Nepali
Papua New Guinea (Pidgin)
Pilipino (Tagalog)
Quechua
Russian
Scandinavian Europe
  *Covers Danish, Finnish, Icelandic,
  Norwegian and Swedish*
South-East Asia
  *Covers Burmese, Indonesian, Khmer,
  Lao, Malay, Tagalog (Pilipino), Thai and
  Vietnamese*
Spanish (Castilian)
  *Also includes Basque, Catalan and-
  Galician*
Spanish (Latin American)
Sri Lanka
Swahili
Thai
Thai Hill Tribes
Tibetan
Turkish
Ukrainian
USA
  *Introduction to US English,
  Vernacular, Native American
  languages and Hawaiian*
Vietnamese
Western Europe
  *Useful words and phrases in Basque,
  Catalan, Dutch, French, German,
  Greek, Irish, Italian, Portuguese,
  Scottish Gaelic, Spanish (Castilian) and
  Welsh*

COMPLETE LIST OF LONELY PLANET BOOKS

AFRICA

Africa - the South • Africa on a shoestring • Arabic (Moroccan) phrasebook • Cape Town • Central Africa • East Africa • Egypt • Egypt travel atlas • Ethiopian (Amharic) phrasebook • Kenya • Kenya travel atlas • Malawi, Mozambique & Zambia • Morocco • North Africa • South Africa, Lesotho & Swaziland • South Africa, Lesotho & Swaziland travel atlas • Swahili phrasebook • Trekking in East Africa• West Africa • Zimbabwe, Botswana & Namibia • Zimbabwe, Botswana & Namibia travel atlas

Travel Literature: The Rainbird: A Central African Journey • Songs to an African Sunset: A Zimbabwean Story

ANTARCTICA

Antarctica

AUSTRALIA & THE PACIFIC

Australia • Australian phrasebook • Bushwalking in Australia • Bushwalking in Papua New Guinea • Fiji • Fijian phrasebook • Islands of Australia's Great Barrier Reef • Melbourne • Micronesia • New Caledonia • New South Wales • New Zealand • Northern Territory • Outback Australia • Papua New Guinea • Papua New Guinea phrasebook • Queensland • Rarotonga & the Cook Islands • Samoa • Solomon Islands • South Australia • Sydney • Tahiti & French Polynesia • Tasmania • Tonga • Tramping in New Zealand • Vanuatu • Victoria • Western Australia

Travel Literature: Islands in the Clouds • Sean & David's Long Drive

CENTRAL AMERICA & THE CARIBBEAN

Bermuda • Central America on a shoestring • Costa Rica • Cuba • Eastern Caribbean • Guatemala, Belize & Yucatán: La Ruta Maya • Jamaica

EUROPE

Amsterdam • Austria • Baltics States phrasebook • Britain • Central Europe on a shoestring • Central Europe phrasebook • Czech & Slovak Republics • Denmark • Dublin • Eastern Europe on a shoestring • Eastern Europe phrasebook • Estonia, Latvia & Lithuania • Finland • France • French phrasebook • Germany • German phrasebook • Greece • Greek phrasebook • Hungary • Iceland, Greenland & the Faroe Islands • Ireland • Italian phrasebook • Italy • Lisbon • London • Mediterranean Europe on a shoestring • Mediterranean Europe phrasebook • Paris • Poland • Portugal • Portugal travel atlas • Prague • Russia, Ukraine & Belarus • Russian phrasebook • Scandinavian & Baltic Europe on a shoestring • Scandinavian Europe phrasebook • Slovenia • Spain • Spanish phrasebook • St Petersburg • Switzerland • Trekking in Spain • Ukrainian phrasebook • Vienna • Walking in Britain • Walking in Switzerland • Western Europe on a shoestring • Western Europe phrasebook

Travel Literature: The Olive Grove: Travels in Greece

INDIAN SUBCONTINENT

Bangladesh • Bengali phrasebook • Delhi • Goa • Hindi/Urdu phrasebook • India • India & Bangladesh travel atlas • Indian Himalaya • Karakoram Highway • Nepal • Nepali phrasebook • Pakistan • Rajasthan • Sri Lanka • Sri Lanka phrasebook • Trekking in the Indian Himalaya • Trekking in the Karakoram & Hindukush • Trekking in the Nepal Himalaya

Travel Literature: In Rajasthan • Shopping for Buddhas

COMPLETE LIST OF LONELY PLANET BOOKS

ISLANDS OF THE INDIAN OCEAN
Madagascar & Comoros • Maldives • Mauritius, Réunion & Seychelles

NORTH AMERICA
Alaska • Backpacking in Alaska • Baja California • California & Nevada • Canada • Deep South • Florida • Hawaii • Honolulu • Los Angeles • Mexico • Miami • New England • New Orleans • New York City • New York, New Jersey & Pennsylvania • Pacific Northwest USA • Rocky Mountain States • San Francisco • Southwest USA • USA phrasebook • Washington, DC & the Capital Region
Travel Literature: Drive thru America

NORTH-EAST ASIA
Beijing • Cantonese phrasebook • China • Hong Kong • Hong Kong, Macau & Guangzhou • Japan • Japanese phrasebook • Japanese audio pack • Korea • Korean phrasebook • Mandarin phrasebook • Mongolia • Mongolian phrasebook • North-East Asia on a shoestring • Seoul • Taiwan • Tibet • Tibet phrasebook • Tokyo
Travel Literature: Lost Japan

MIDDLE EAST & CENTRAL ASIA
Arab Gulf States • Arabic (Egyptian) phrasebook • Cairo • Central Asia • Central Asia phrasebook • Iran • Israel & the Palestinian Territories • Israel & the Palestinian Territories travel atlas • Istanbul • Jerusalem • Jordan & Syria • Jordan, Syria & Lebanon travel atlas • Lebanon • Middle East • Turkey • Turkish phrasebook • Turkey travel atlas • Yemen
Travel Literature: The Gates of Damascus • Kingdom of the Film Stars: Journey into Jordan

SOUTH AMERICA
Argentina, Uruguay & Paraguay • Bolivia • Brazil • Brazilian phrasebook • Buenos Aires • Chile & Easter Island • Chile & Easter Island travel atlas • Colombia • Ecuador & the Galápagos Islands • Latin American Spanish phrasebook • Peru • Quechua phrasebook • Rio de Janeiro • South America on a shoestring • Trekking in the Patagonian Andes • Venezuela
Travel Literature: Full Circle: A South American Journey

SOUTH-EAST ASIA
Bali & Lombok • Bangkok • Burmese phrasebook • Cambodia • Ho Chi Minh City • Indonesia • Indonesian phrasebook • Indonesian audio pack • Jakarta • Java • Laos • Laos travel atlas • Lao phrasebook • Malay phrasebook • Malaysia, Singapore & Brunei • Myanmar (Burma) • Philippines • Pilipino phrasebook • Singapore • South-East Asia on a shoestring • South-East Asia phrasebook • Thailand • Thailand's Islands & Beaches • Thailand travel atlas • Thai phrasebook • Thai Hill Tribes phrasebook • Thai audio pack • Vietnam • Vietnamese phrasebook • Vietnam travel atlas

For ordering information contact your nearest Lonely Planet office.

PLANET TALK

Lonely Planet's FREE quarterly newsletter

Every issue is packed with up-to-date travel news
and advice including:

- a letter from Lonely Planet co-founders Tony and
  Maureen Wheeler
- go behind the scenes on the road with a Lonely
  Planet author
- feature article on an important and topical travel
  issue
- a selection of recent letters from travellers
- details on forthcoming Lonely Planet promotions
- complete list of Lonely Planet products

To join our mailing list contact any Lonely Planet office.

LONELY PLANET PUBLICATIONS

AUSTRALIA
PO Box 617, Hawthorn 3122, Victoria
tel: (03) 9819 1877 fax: (03) 9819 6459
e-mail: talk2us@lonelyplanet.com.au

USA
Embarcadero West,
155 Filbert St, Suite 251,
Oakland, CA 94607
tel: (510) 893 8555
TOLL FREE: 800 275-8555
fax: (510) 893 8563
e-mail: info@lonelyplanet.com

UK
10a Spring Place,
London NW5 3BH
tel: (0171) 428 2800 fax: (0171) 428 4828
e-mail: go@lonelyplanet.co.uk

FRANCE:
71 bis rue du Cardinal Lemoine, 75005
Paris
tel: 1 44 32 06 20 fax: 1 46 34 72 55
e-mail: 100560.415@compuserve.com

**World Wide Web: http://www.lonelyplanet.com
or AOL keyword: lp**